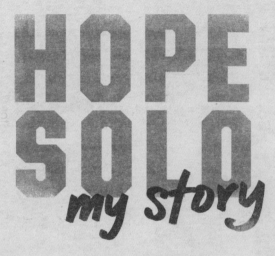

HOPE SOLO
my story

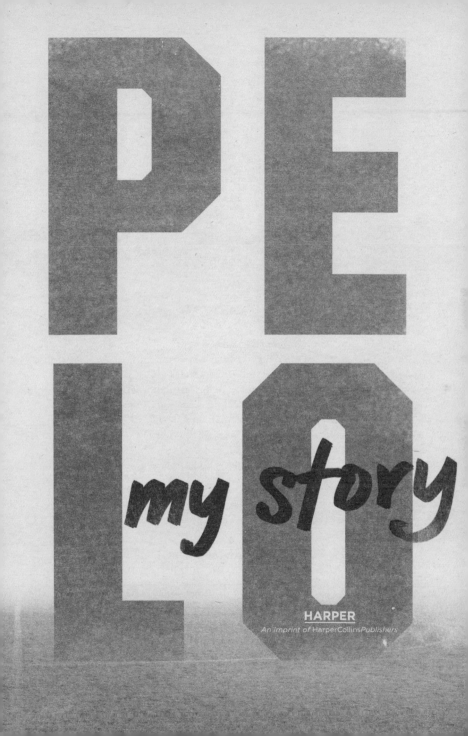

PE
LO

my *story*

HARPER
An Imprint of HarperCollinsPublishers

Hope Solo: My Story

Copyright © 2012 by Hope Solo

www.harpercollinschildrens.com

ISBN 978-0-06-222066-0

16 17   OPM   10 9 8 7 6
❖
First paperback edition, 2013

To my mom, the true champion

CONTENTS

	Prologue	1
Chapter 1	LIFE BEHIND THE SMILEY FACE	3
Chapter 2	GOD'S SECOND PARADISE	12
Chapter 3	A DOUBLE IDENTITY	23
Chapter 4	SOMEWHERE—ANYWHERE—FAR AWAY	32
Chapter 5	BARE-BRANCHED BUT READY TO BLOOM	41
Chapter 6	THE '99ERS	55
Chapter 7	"I SHOULD HAVE DIED A LONG TIME AGO"	69
Chapter 8	AN ARM LIKE FRANKENSTEIN	78
Chapter 9	MADE IN THE WUSA	90
Chapter 10	BAA, BAA, BLACK SHEEP	102
Chapter 11	"ONLY A DAUGHTER CRIES LIKE THAT"	115
Chapter 12	SHADOWS	125

Chapter 13	"YOU CAN'T GO BY A GUT FEELING"	131
Chapter 14	STEPPING INTO LIQUID	149
Chapter 15	"DON'T LET THE DEVIL STEAL YOUR JOY"	162
Chapter 16	THE NEW #1	172
Chapter 17	PRETTY SWEET	188
Chapter 18	UNPROFESSIONAL PROFESSIONALS	192
Chapter 19	SEATTLE'S FINEST	198
Chapter 20	IT JUST TAKES ONE	208
Chapter 21	THE SILVER LINING	218
Chapter 22	FAIRY-TALE ENDING	228
Acknowledgments		239
Questions and Answers		243

PROLOGUE

I DON'T BELIEVE ANY ENDING is ever completely happy.
But maybe my mother did back when I was born. She
had known a popular older girl in high school named
Hope, who had been kind to her, and for her the name
was filled with a sense of friendship and belonging.
My father said he viewed my birth as a fresh start, a
chance for him to leave something good in a world
that had brought him mostly trouble and bad luck.

  Hope.

1

LIFE BEHIND THE SMILEY FACE

I GREW UP IN A tract house on Marshall Street in Richland, Washington.

My earliest memories are filled with happiness: A small red house with a wooden fence; my free-spirited mother, Judy; my big, outgoing father, Gerry; my older brother, Marcus; and me, Baby Hope.

On the outside of the fence, for everyone passing by to see, was a giant yellow smiley face. On the other side was a yard with a sandbox and a jungle gym. An English sheepdog named Charlotte. Rabbits and turtles and kittens. Out back we played Red Light, Green Light and had Easter egg hunts and birthday parties. Inside the house, my mother, a budding photographer, set up a darkroom to develop film, as well as a workout room where she practiced karate. I snuggled with my parents in their bed and watched TV. The cozy kitchen was where we had family spaghetti dinners.

Smiley face on the fence, happy people in the house.

But the truth is a little more complicated. Clutter—plastic toys, yard equipment, bikes, an old, beat-up car—filled up our side yard. The neighbors complained, so my parents were forced to put up a fence to hide it all. My mom didn't like thinking the neighbors had won some kind of victory, so she painted that yellow happy face as tall and as wide as the fence would allow. The smiley face wasn't about happiness but a protest against our neighbors.

My mother came to Richland because of the nuclear reactors. With neat rows of streets along the banks of the Columbia River, Richland looks like a normal American town. But it has a complex history.

During World War II, the U.S. government started the Manhattan Project to create the first atomic bomb. They wanted to continue the project in secret. They forced the relocation of about 1,500 residents from Hanford, a small farming community near Seattle, and built a 586-square-mile nuclear campus there. Workers were brought in and housed in tent barracks and, later, in small tract houses in nearby Richland. The workforce grew to 51,000, and three nuclear reactors were producing the plutonium that was used to build some of the first atomic bombs. No one was allowed to speak of it: Husbands and wives weren't even allowed to tell each other what their jobs were. Residents hung blackout curtains at night and spoke in whispers inside their own homes. There were signs posted in public places: CARELESS TALK COSTS LIVES.

Old-timers tell stories handed down over the years, of neighbors seen chatting in public before abruptly disappearing without so much as a good-bye. The secretive origins of Richland became a part of our ordinary lives.

On August 9, 1945, the first atomic bomb was dropped on Nagasaki, Japan. Although it is often considered to mark the end of World War II, the use of such a powerful bomb that caused so much pain and destruction was also a dark moment in human history.

My family actually didn't help make the bomb. It wasn't until 1969, long after World War II, that my grandfather, Pete Shaw, and Grandma Alice moved to Washington with their four children.

How did my father come to Richland? I wish I

knew the entire answer to that question.

Here's what I do know: My mother, who had moved to Everett, Washington, as a young woman, married my father and became pregnant with me while my father was serving a prison sentence. My brother, Marcus, was a toddler at the time. Overwhelmed, my mother had no choice but to move in with her parents in Richland. My father followed after his release. He and my mother eventually set up house behind the smiley-face fence, a few blocks from my grandparents.

I was born on a hot, dry day in the middle of summer: July 30, 1981. My father chose that day to bring his other two children from his first marriage to Richland for a visit. My half brother, David, was twelve, and my half sister, Terry, was nine. My mother brought me—her new baby, Hope Amelia Solo— home from the hospital to a chaotic house with three young children. Things never really got any calmer.

David and Terry lived in Kirkland, Washington— just outside of Seattle, on the other side of the mountains—with their mother. They came to visit every summer and sometimes went camping with us. They learned to call my grandparents Grandma and Grandpa. I didn't realize until I was much older how hard our mothers worked to make sure the four of us could feel like a family.

Terry adored me. She liked to dress me up, but as I got older, I resisted. I was an active, grubby little kid. I didn't want to wear dresses. I didn't like dolls. I liked to play outside, wear an oversize Orange Crush hat, and do whatever Marcus was doing.

If he ran, I ran. If he played baseball, I played baseball. If he rode his skateboard, I wanted to ride his skateboard—not mine, *his*, because mine was hot pink and girly and his was so much cooler. Even as a little girl, I was tough and strong. One day I took Marcus's skateboard to the top of the little hill across from our house and rode down. I smashed into our bikes, which were lying in the driveway. A pedal gashed my chin, and blood splashed everywhere. I was running in circles to distract myself from the pain as the blood gushed through my fingers. I had to go to the emergency room and get stitched up.

Marcus and his friends would challenge me to pull them in a wagon. And I could do it, pull all three of them. When my mom went on a bike ride, I would run alongside her, chatting, never getting winded. My father and I would play basketball against Marcus and David. My dad would have to lift me up toward the hoop so I could shoot. I loved to play Wiffle ball and hated losing, determined to play until I won.

Luckily for me, I was growing up in a time when active little girls could finally turn to organized sports. That wasn't the case for my grandma, who had loved speed skating while she was a girl in Duluth, Minnesota. Or for my mother—a wiry, athletic woman who loved karate and waterskiing. In the early 1980s, youth soccer was growing fast everywhere. It was my first organized sport, starting in kindergarten. I had no problem scoring goals, even as a five-year-old. We were the Pink Panthers, my dad was a coach, and I always played forward. I would dribble through all the other kids and score. It was easy for me, and fun.

My mother was working at Hanford by then, testing plutonium samples on rotating shifts. She was exhausted a lot of the time. My father stayed home, taking care of Marcus and me. He worked on and off, sometimes doing counseling for troubled youth. My early memories of my father are of a loving, loud, larger-than-life man—six foot three with a huge belly and a big laugh. He had jet-black hair and tattooed arms—a skull and crossbones on one bicep, a mermaid on one forearm, and my mother's name, JUDY LYNN SOLO, on the other.

To him, I was always Baby Hope. We had a special bond. I remember riding on his shoulders and stroking his thick black hair. I remember wrestling on the floor with him, his big round belly shaking with laughter. He helped teach me to read. On Christmas he dressed up as Santa. He was a popular youth coach—my soccer teammates loved him. He also coached all my brother's sports teams—baseball, basketball, soccer—and all the kids adored Coach Gerry. Sports were his passion: In our house we loved the Oakland Raiders, the Red Sox, and the University of Washington football teams, which made us stand out in an area loyal to the Seahawks, the Mariners, and Washington State.

When my dad was around, we would share tubs of Neapolitan ice cream—although he ate all the strawberry—while we watched TV. We'd go to 7-Eleven and get white-powdered doughnuts and Slurpees, mixing up all the different flavors.

But as I got older, I started to see that my life wasn't as perfect as it seemed. One spring, when I was a Brownie, the Girl Scout cookie money went missing. Sometimes my father went missing. One morning, my mother went out to get her car and it was gone: repossessed for lack of payment.

One afternoon when I was about five or six, my parents and grandfather stood outside in our driveway, having an intense conversation. "Come inside, Hope," Grandma said. "Come on, Marcus."

We sat at the kitchen table, with an Etch A Sketch between us. "What else can you draw on that?" Grandma asked as soon as we finished a picture. She was trying to distract us from what was going on outside, but I could hear the angry voices. I knew something bad was happening. Grandpa Pete was very upset as he talked to my parents behind the smiley face.

Later I learned that my father had taken my grandfather's checkbook out of my grandparents' home and stolen $1,800 by writing checks to himself.

My father moved out the next day. I didn't get to say good-bye—he asked my mother if he could pick me up from school, but I was going to a friend's house, so he said good-bye only to Marcus. For years I felt guilty that I didn't say good-bye to my father that day.

A short time later, we had to leave the smiley-face house because my father had never paid the mortgage.

After we lost our house, we moved into a duplex in a low-rent part of Richland with my mother. We still had occasional contact with my father. My mother didn't bar him from our lives because she knew how much we loved him.

He would promise to come and take us out for ice cream or come to our soccer games, and then he wouldn't show. I remember waiting hours for him. Sometimes he would give me a card with a check inside, and I would ask my mother if the check was any good. Even as a little girl, I was learning not to take things at face value.

When I was about eight years old, my father left

Washington, and I didn't see him for a very long time.

It's a complicated thing, knowing how much pain my father caused in my life and the lives of others, yet still holding love for him in my heart. No matter what he did, he was my father. He helped create the person I am. He showered me with love; he just didn't know how to be a husband or a father or a responsible member of society.

If I hadn't made peace with him later in my life, I'd still be bitter and angry.

2

GOD'S SECOND PARADISE

MY MOTHER MARRIED MY STEPFATHER, Glenn, on the Columbia River on a beautiful March day in 1989. I was wearing a polka-dot dress that matched the one worn by my new stepsister, Connie. She was Glenn's daughter from his first marriage, three years older than me. Two boats were tethered together, bobbing on the current. I stood rocking gently on the calm water, proud and happy to be part of the ceremony.

But the calm didn't make it ashore. Glenn tried to instill order—I know now he was trying to do the right thing, but Marcus and I weren't interested in a new father, or new rules. And we didn't have a vote in the matter. Glenn was a no-nonsense man—six foot six, more than three hundred pounds, with a voice as rumbly as the truck engines he worked on. He barked orders at Marcus and me, made up rules, occasionally even tried to spank us. We had never been treated like that. Before Glenn came along, we had been free to do what we pleased, latchkey kids dependent only on each other, with a mother constantly working to support us. Now we had more order, more stability, but also more tension and anger.

It was only about four months after the wedding when my father dropped out of our lives. He simply vanished, leaving behind a gaping hole.

Our resentment of Glenn quickly filled the void.

Things were especially hard on my brother.

Marcus took after my father—dark-haired, dark-eyed, and big. When Marcus was a child, one boy teased him about being fat. When Marcus was in seventh grade, he beat the kid up, bad enough to send him to the hospital.

With that fight, Marcus was branded. He was a tough guy, a target of local police, viewed as a threat by teachers and parents.

There was another side of him, though. He was a good athlete and had lots of friends in the popular crowd. He had a kind heart and would defend kids who were outcasts. Every morning he gave a mentally challenged neighbor a ride to school.

But Marcus never backed down from a confrontation, and by the time he got to high school, his reputation was firmly established all over town. You didn't mess with Marcus Solo.

And like Marcus, I was gaining a reputation. When I was in fourth grade I saw a bully picking on my classmate, a nerdy kid who couldn't defend himself. I was furious. I pushed the bully off his bike and punched him in the face. The school principal called my mother, and I was suspended from after-school sports for a few days. The boy's family was outraged that a girl had beaten up their son.

That was the first time I remember getting in real trouble at school, but it wasn't the last time. I was trying to prove myself to Marcus. He was my closest family member and my protector. He walked me home from school, kept me company, made me laugh. We were strongly connected, the only ones who understood what we'd been through. We would sometimes fight each other, but pity the outsider who tried to mess with us. And the outsider in our house was Glenn.

Usually, Marcus and I escaped to our grandparents' house. Grandma Alice and Grandpa Pete had a sign by their front door: GRANDKIDS WELCOME. And they meant it. When we showed up, we were always let in, no questions asked. We could get a snack or play a board game or just tip back in one of their big recliners and watch TV. It was calm at my grandparents'. They loved us unconditionally.

Grandpa Pete was brilliant; he'd earned his electrical engineering degree from USC after serving in the navy. He managed the engineering unit at Hanford until he retired in 1988. Grandma said she married him because he was the only man she'd met who was smarter than she was. He always seemed happiest when he was out on the river, at the wheel of his boat. Every Christmas, Grandpa would decorate the boat for the parade of lights with a lighted tree, a star, and a cross he had welded together. He would let me steer the boat and get on the intercom to say, "Ho, ho, ho—merrrrrrry Christmas!" We liked to walk down to the river together with his black Lab, Maggie, and throw the rubber toy into the water for her. Grandpa could always make me laugh with one of his jokes, even if I had been in tears just moments before.

Grandma Alice was the rock of the family, making sure we all went to Sunday school, that we had enough pocket money, and that we had a place to stay if we needed to get away from home. My grandparents were spiritual people—they pastored at a church in nearby Mabton. Grandpa sang in the choir, Grandma gave sermons, and we helped clean up after the services. It felt like our own little family church. I went with Grandma to deliver flowers to nursing homes and to funerals. I walked up to caskets with her to say good-bye—I was never afraid of dead bodies because Grandma seemed so at peace with them. My grandparents set an example for how to treat others and withhold judgment; they cared for disabled adults and opened their home to those in need. They loved to travel: to Germany for the Passion play in Oberammergau and to the Holy Land in Israel for pilgrimages. Grandma Alice called Richland "God's second paradise" because the stark desert plateau reminded her of Israel.

Grandma explained that every stress and strain in life was the Lord's will. She peppered her conversation with bits of Christian thought. She told me, "Don't let the devil steal your joy." She loved my name and once told me, "Hope is, by definition, defiant. It is only when everything is hopeless that hope begins to be a strength."

Grandma and Grandpa showed up for all our sporting events and school activities. They took me to soccer tournaments in their camper, setting up chairs and playing cards while they waited between games. Their house was our shelter—a place to escape Glenn. We'd stay there until my mother could convince us to come home, promising that Glenn would be cool. We'd go home for a while, and then the chaos would start again, and we'd run the four blocks back to Grandma and Grandpa.

My mother was working full-time at Hanford. When I entered middle school, Hanford had shifted into cleanup mode. The government had to deal with the massive amounts of hazardous waste left behind from the nuclear buildup of the Cold War. This kept Richland citizens employed. Mom was working to clean up what has been called the most toxic site in the world. And the environment after work was pretty toxic too.

Every conversation became a battle. If my mom tried to discipline me or offer advice, I would attack her for her own failures. I felt like the outsider in my own house. My mother seemed more concerned with Marcus than with me. He demanded more attention: He was in constant trouble. I was lower maintenance: younger, a good student, busy with sports and my social life. But I felt neglected. I didn't have my father. I rebelled against my stepfather. And I felt I couldn't depend on my mother. At night, lying in bed, I made up stories about running away to Seattle to find my dad. We'd watch sports and eat Neapolitan ice cream—he could have all the strawberry.

My sister, Terry, decided I needed a female

influence. Ten years older than me, she was a young woman with her own busy life, but she stayed connected, driving over the mountains to visit whenever she could. When she went on a trip to New York, she sent me fashionable gifts, like a pink Swatch watch. One day she picked me up and took me back to Seattle for a girls' weekend. I was thrilled.

Terry is beautiful, dark-haired and stylish. When I was young, I was in awe of her looks and fashion sense. On that weekend in Seattle, she tried to spoil me and smooth down my rough edges. I loved the attention. She took me shopping at Nordstrom's department store and bought me a green dress covered in little white flowers, along with green suede shoes. I twirled in front of the mirror and admired the way I looked. I hadn't worn a dress in years—since my mother's wedding to Glenn. I usually just wore a dirty old Raiders hoodie, with my hair pulled back in a ponytail.

But in that fancy downtown Seattle department store, I liked what I saw in the mirror. I felt beautiful.

We went to a skin-care salon, where I got a facial. Terry shaped and tweezed my eyebrows. Then, all dressed up and made over, we went to the Space Needle restaurant for dinner. The Space Needle was like our Eiffel Tower. Being there meant you were someplace important and sophisticated, high above everything else.

From atop the Space Needle, I looked out over the city and felt like a princess, like Dorothy in the Emerald City. I felt so lucky to have a big sister who was so kind. While the rest of the Solo children had inherited our father's hot temper and short fuse, Terry was a peacemaker. She knew that things were difficult for me at home, that I needed to feel safe.

When I got back to Richland, I was teased because my eyebrows looked too perfect. But my best friend, Cheryl, told me I looked pretty. I could always count on her.

She and I had met in third grade. I'd started playing on a new recreation-league soccer team and met a little blond girl named Cheryl Gies on the first day of practice. Pretty soon we were inseparable. Cheryl and Hope, Hope and Cheryl—for the next ten years.

Cheryl was one of the only people I let get close. She was allowed into my house, inside my crazy life, an eyewitness to the chaos. She saw it all. She didn't pass judgment or criticize. I think she knew things were weird in my house and minded coming over, but she didn't want to hurt my feelings. She remained my friend, no matter what she witnessed. When I didn't feel like a normal kid, I took comfort in having a normal best friend.

Cheryl lived on the other side of town, in a new development of large homes on Appaloosa Way. At

Cheryl's house, no one was screaming or fighting. There were framed pictures of her family on the walls, pleasant-smelling candles in the bathroom, and no clutter in the hallway. Even their garage was neatly organized. Being at Cheryl's was like traveling into another universe. I started to spend almost as much time there as I did at home.

Cheryl's parents, Mary and Dick, were generous. They invited me to spend the night all the time. They could see past my tough front. They could tell I was a good kid. Their biggest concern was my risk taking: I was always the first one to jump off a cliff into the river, to try to swim out to an island, to leap between balconies at a motel where we were staying with our soccer team. I urged Cheryl to keep up with me.

I wasn't intimidated by much. Why should I have been? I was coping with risk and threat on a daily basis at home.

In middle school, I was assigned to write a paper about what I wanted to be when I grew up. It was then that I decided: *I am going to be a professional soccer player.*

I was dreaming for something that didn't even exist. This was years before the 1996 Summer Olympics, when the U.S. women's soccer team first entered the nation's consciousness. This was long before any kind of professional women's league had been established.

I didn't even know the names Mia Hamm or Michelle Akers. I didn't have any role models. But I knew how soccer made me feel, and that I wanted to hold on to that feeling for the rest of my life.

Life was calm and ordered on the soccer field. I was special. My strength and aggression were a plus—I dominated as a forward. Back then, no coach would have ever considered taking me off the field and sticking me in goal. I was a playmaker. Sure, if our team needed a goalkeeper, I was perfectly willing to fill in for a half. But I was too good an athlete to be goalie. That was where the slow girls played, the uncoordinated ones who couldn't run or score. I was a goal-scoring machine, always leading the attack. I felt free and unburdened.

In middle school, our soccer team jumped up to another level. The core group had been together for years—pretty much since the day I met Cheryl— with our coach, Carl Wheeler. We became a "select" team, which meant a higher level of competition and commitment. We were expected to travel to tournaments. And there were costs involved, which made it difficult for my family. I was fortunate that Cheryl was my teammate. Mary and Dick drove me to tournaments, took me out to eat, and never made me feel as though I didn't have enough. My coaches, Carl and later Tim Atencio, gave me rides and helped me out, buying snacks and Gatorade if I didn't have anything with me.

Our team traveled around the state to play. We loved beating the top teams in Seattle. They were the big-city kids who were supposed to win. We were the scrappy country kids who showed up in T-shirts with numbers instead of fancy jerseys. When we beat those rich-kid teams, it felt awesome.

One autumn Sunday, we were on the other side of the mountains for a game. It was a dark, rainy day, and Cheryl and I had carpooled with another player's family. We pulled up in the parking lot next to the field, which was in the middle of a park, surrounded by woods and dripping trees. I got out of the car and looked around for our coach. Then I saw a large man limping through the parking lot in a rumpled trench coat.

I dropped my bag. "Cheryl," I said, "I think that's my dad."

3

A DOUBLE IDENTITY

MY HEART THUDDED AS I walked across the parking lot. There was no doubt in my mind who this man was, even though it had been five years since I'd last seen him.

He stopped walking. We looked at each other and—for a beat—I wondered if he would even recognize me. "Baby Hope," he said. He opened his arms to wrap me in a hug.

I stepped forward into his embrace. Of course my father recognized me. I was still his Baby Hope. It didn't matter how much time had passed. I wanted to ask him a thousand questions, tell him a million things. But I didn't know where to start. I felt shy and nervous.

"Cheryl," I said. "This is my dad."

My dad. The words tasted funny in my mouth.

During our warm-ups, Cheryl and I tried to impress him. Our ongoing goal was to break the team record for number of times heading the ball—usually we could get around seventy headers back and forth without letting the ball touch the ground. That day, heading to each other while my father watched, we broke the record, keeping the ball in the air for eighty-eight touches.

I wanted to play the game of my life on that muddy field that day in Seattle. I wanted to show my very first soccer coach what a strong player I was. My father loved sports. I wanted him to see what kind of athlete I was becoming. I was like a puppy, amped up and eager to show off, and once the game began, I channeled that onto the field. In the first half, I scored on a header, and then scored two more times. In the second half, we had a healthy lead, so we rotated goalkeepers, and I went into goal. I slipped going for a ball, and my opponent chipped it over my head and into the net. My dad never let me forget that: The first time he ever saw me play in goal, I let in a sky ball.

Happy and sweating, I went over to my father

when the game ended.

"Would you like to see where I live, Baby Hope?" my father asked.

Absolutely. I motioned for Cheryl to come with me, and we followed my father as he limped down the path that led into the woods. It was wet and dark, and our footsteps were quiet on the damp earth. I wasn't scared, just curious. To the right of the path, we spotted a blue tarp set up like a tent, covering some belongings. My father stopped in front of the makeshift shelter. "This is where I live," he said.

My father was homeless. His few possessions were inside a duffel bag, stuck under the blue tarp to stay dry. There was no one else around, just one man's lonely spot in the rain-soaked woods. I hadn't had much experience with homeless people, yet I wasn't completely shocked. My father was such a mystery, he could have flown us to the moon and told me he lived there and I would have believed him.

Cheryl was more unnerved than I was. I think that was the moment she fully realized how different my family life was from hers.

It was time to go even though I wanted to stay and spend more time with my father, we had a long drive back to Richland. We hugged good-bye.

"Dad, come see me play basketball sometime," I begged.

"I will, Baby Hope," he said.

How did my father end up at the same field where I was playing? I never found out. Maybe he saw that a Tri-Cities soccer team was scheduled for a game and thought there was a possibility I'd be there. Maybe it was just chance. Or maybe it was fate.

That sky ball I let in while my dad was watching didn't bother me. I wasn't a goalkeeper. I was just goofing around, doing my coach a favor. He wanted to let the regular keeper out to play in the field after we had established a healthy lead. And that lead was usually because of my goal scoring. I was a standout field player.

When I was thirteen, I went an hour north to Moses Lake for tryouts for the Eastern Washington Olympic Development Program. Olympic development programs target the top young soccer players in each age group by area. The road to the women's national team begins in youth ODP. But that road can be an expensive one: ODP costs a lot of money—for travel, uniforms, and coaching. But I wasn't thinking about any of that when I went to Moses Lake. All the best players from the east side of the Cascades were there, their registration numbers written in black Sharpie on their arms and legs. Looking around, I realized how many strong players were in my age group, and I started to get worried that I might not make the team.

For one of the first times in my life, I felt insecure on the soccer field.

There was a shortage of goalkeepers—there almost always is. Talented athletes—the kind who make up the ODP—are reluctant to commit to the position. Goalkeeping isn't glamorous. It's tough and stressful and thankless. And in youth soccer, players see that the less athletic kids are stuck in goal, creating a stigma about goalkeeping. But some of the coaches evaluating the ODP players had already seen me play the position. At a club tournament in Oregon when our regular goalkeeper was injured, I had filled in, and I was good at it. I was a strong athlete, and playing basketball had honed my hand-eye coordination and leaping skills—traits that not all soccer players possess.

"Hope Solo," a coach called. "We'd like to take a look at you with the goalkeepers."

I was game—I just wanted to make the team. I batted away shots and dove to make saves. I was chosen. But then an older team—three levels up— decided they wanted me for a backup goalkeeper and cherry-picked me off my age-group team. That was flattering. So there I was, a scrawny little thirteen year-old, playing on an under-sixteen team with girls who were much more mature. Amy Allmann, coach of the regional ODP team and a former national team goalkeeper, didn't think I was anything special the first time she saw me play. Then she realized I was playing against girls who were three years older. All of a sudden, she was intrigued.

The older players were sweet to me. They did my hair and made me wear lip gloss, and we listened to Shania Twain's "Any Man of Mine" over and over again on the CD player. I was their baby sister, just a lanky little thing among the tall trees. I liked the status of playing above my age group, and I was good in goal because I was athletic and fearless. But still, I didn't want to be a goalkeeper. I wanted to touch the ball, to attack. Now I stood in the net, watching the action running away from me, waiting for my turn to do something.

My family hated watching me play goalkeeper and let everyone know it, complaining loudly. My mother and grandmother thought I was being robbed of my true talent. They were also convinced I was going to get hurt in a collision with girls who had already reached their full maturity.

Their concern was valid. The first time I played with my new ODP team, I replaced the starting goalkeeper, who had just suffered a concussion in a collision in the net. As she was carted away in an ambulance, I pulled on my oversized goalkeeper jersey and giant gloves and went into battle. My mother and grandmother covered their eyes. I was nervous, but I prided myself on my ability to rise to a challenge. And I did.

After that, I started living a dual soccer life. For my club and eventually my high school teams, I was always a forward, a goal scorer my teammates relied on to win the game. But at the ODP level, I was always a goalkeeper, the one my teammates needed to save the game. The two roles kept me interested and challenged and also helped my soccer development. I learned both ends of the field. Knowing how a forward attacks is an advantage for a goalkeeper. It was as if I had a double identity—my Richland life and my expanding outside world as a successful goalkeeper.

By the time I got to Richland High, I already had a target on my back. I was a standout soccer player. I was a Solo. I wasn't going to blend in. As a freshman starter on the varsity soccer team, I scored seventeen goals and got attention from reporters, who loved making puns out of my name: I was trying to win games "solo" or was giving my team "hope."

Marcus was a senior when I was a freshman. He'd been in trouble a lot throughout high school. His coaches and some of the teachers at Richland loved him, but others hated and feared him. The same was true for the students—there was no middle ground with Marcus. When I got to Richland High, I sensed teachers and administrators eyeing me, thinking, *Oh no, here comes another Solo.* I, too, split people into camps: They either loved me or hated me, even though I wasn't a troublemaker. I got good grades. I made the honor roll every semester of high school and kept my grade-point average at 3.8 for four years.

Meanwhile, my fighting with my mother was getting worse. I had little respect for my mother or Glenn, so I refused to acknowledge their rules. One day Glenn had enough of my defiance. "If you don't like it, get out," he shouted at me.

"I will!" I screamed.

And I did. First I went to my grandparents' for a few weeks. Then—encouraged by my forgiving grandma to give Mom and Glenn another shot—I went back home. But it was still unbearable.

"Cheryl," I cried to my best friend, "I don't know what to do. I can't live with them."

"Why don't you come stay with me?" Cheryl said.

She checked with her parents, who, as always, welcomed me into their home. At the time, Cheryl's middle brother and Mary had moved to Iowa for a few months for Mary's work, and her oldest brother was in college. So it was just me and Dick and Cheryl. Cheryl was more than happy to have my company.

But eventually I went home to my family. It was hard, but I told myself that all of this was making me tougher. I was proud of all these challenges and fiercely protective of my strange family tree. I was a survivor.

4

SOMEWHERE– ANYWHERE– FAR AWAY

ONE EVENING, MY MOM AND Glenn called me into the living room and told me to sit down.

Uh-oh. What had I done this time?

"Hope, we don't think you can play ODP this year," Glenn said.

I stared at him in shock. I was in high school, and I'd already been playing in the Olympic Development Program for years. I was being scouted by top college coaches.

"It's just very expensive," my mother said. She looked unhappy. My mother had been laid off from Hanford.

I understood that finances were a strain. But how could they think about taking away the most important part of my life? Soccer was my way out, how I was going to make it in the world. Between club soccer and high school soccer, I played seven days a week, and as soon as the fall soccer season ended, I played varsity basketball. In the spring and summer, there were ODP tournaments. I was working hard with a goal in sight—a college, one far away. The recruiting letters were filling up our mailbox. I loved counting them, eager to accumulate more and more. They validated all my sweat and hard work. I kept the letters in two big binders, and I often shut my bedroom door and flipped through them, envisioning my escape. I imagined what the schools were like, how I'd look in the team uniform, how it would feel walking across campus somewhere far, far away, maybe North Carolina or California. I would leave Richland behind.

And now they wanted to take it away from me. "You can't do this to me!" I shouted. "This is my life. This is how I'm going to go to college."

Glenn and my mom didn't say anything. I think they were surprised at the intensity of my reaction and realized, maybe for the first time, the depth of my passion and commitment. I ran into my room, slammed the door, and sobbed. If I couldn't play ODP,

I couldn't get a college scholarship. I was going to be stuck in Richland my entire life. I was probably going to end up working at Hanford, cleaning up nuclear waste.

But my fears were unfounded. I lived in a community that was proud of its athletes. Without my knowing, several people in the community had already helped me out financially, chipping in over the years to make sure I could play club soccer for the Three Rivers Soccer Club, pay the tournament fees, stay in hotels, and travel to away games. My first coach, Carl Wheeler, helped out. So did Tim Atencio, who aided me in raising money to play ODP. After that conversation with my mother and Glenn, I set about raising money myself. It was humbling—soliciting money at local tournaments and asking my club for help. But people seemed to take pride in giving me a hand; my Richland neighbors were invested in my athletic success.

I was able to keep playing. And eventually, the state and regional programs found money for me. My soccer career wasn't going to end.

It was a good time to be a female athlete. The summer before my sophomore year, the Atlanta Olympics were dubbed the Women's Games. American female athletes—including the U.S. women's soccer team—stole the show. This success showed how well Title

IX had worked. Title IX is a federal law that passed in 1972, nine years before I was born. It bans gender discrimination in places funded by the federal government. What it meant was that public schools legally had to provide equal opportunities in sports for boys and girls. Before Title IX, a high school might have had a boys' soccer team but no girls' team. After Title IX, public high school athletics always included girls' teams. By the time I was in high school, the first generation to grow up under Title IX was winning fistfuls of gold medals.

The U.S. soccer team drew huge crowds that summer as they made their gold-medal run. It was the first time most people had ever heard of such players as Mia Hamm, Julie Foudy, and Michelle Akers, and their popularity was rooted in soccer-playing kids like me all over the country.

But Title IX didn't make things easier inside my house. Money continued to be a touchy subject, and I looked to my friends for extra support.

Cheryl and I had been friends since we were children, but I soon found another best friend in Liz Duncan. Liz and I had a friendship that had grown from mutual interests. She was a year older than me and also played both basketball and soccer. She was fiercely competitive but dorky and funny off the court. She was beautiful and dated the best football player at our high school, but like me, she wasn't locked into the popular group. I looked up to her and was happy when she went out of her way to befriend me.

Liz was a midfielder and assisted on many of my goals. Off the field, we were a team as well—we were two jocks dating football players that all the popular girls wanted. We were both nominated every year for homecoming princess but didn't win. It was our annual joke—we thought about getting each other fake tiaras. Finally, her senior year, Liz won. A year later, I did, too.

Our high school soccer team had become a force. We made it to the state championships twice, losing in the semifinals my sophomore year and winning it all in my senior year. I finished my high school soccer career with 109 goals, 38 scored in my senior year. The parents and players helped construct a new soccer field next to Richland High so we didn't have to travel across town to play. The football players dragged couches from Goodwill out to the field and sat on them, wearing matching yellow shirts, proclaiming themselves the Bleacher Bums. When we made it to the state finals, it seemed that our whole town drove over the mountains to Seattle to attend, caravanning in buses and cars.

In basketball, Richland went from having a losing program to being a regional contender. We had a two-story gym—with a mushroom cloud painted on the middle of the court—and our games were packed with fans, many hanging over the top balcony. We made it to the state semifinals my junior year. I was an aggressive basketball player, stealing the ball at will and not fearing contact. Suddenly I was getting recruiting letters from schools that were promising to let me play both sports.

All the state semifinals and championships were played just outside Seattle. My father came to those games. Marcus picked him up in downtown Seattle, drove him to the games, and then dropped him back off on the streets afterward.

In the winter of my junior year, I was named a *Parade* magazine All-American as a goalkeeper. I made the U-17 (under-seventeen) national team, which was coached by April Heinrichs. She had been a national team assistant coach when the United States won gold in Atlanta. I went to train with the team in Chula Vista, California, and played a tournament in Florida. April told me I was the top goalkeeper in camp. All around the country, coaches were now noticing me: the up-and-coming goalkeeper who trained at the position only half the time.

The recruiting letters started to get serious. And I was beginning to understand that goalkeeping was going to be my ticket. Some coaches promised I could also be a field player, and others dangled basketball as well as an incentive. But it was clear that my big selling point was my ability in the net.

I didn't know what I wanted out of college. When asked by local reporters, one day I would say, "It's been a lifelong dream to go to Portland or North Carolina." Another day I'd say, "It's my dream to play at Stanford, but Santa Clara is very interested." What did I know? I just wanted to go to college: somewhere—anywhere—far away. All I knew about North Carolina was that it had a strong women's soccer team: The Tar Heels had won fourteen national championships and the school put players like Mia Hamm on the national team.

Other schools were interested in me. Portland was a long-standing good team that was the pride of the Northwest. Stanford had a top program and was flooding my mailbox with letters. April Heinrichs was the head coach at Virginia and was recruiting me hard. And then there was Lesle Gallimore at the University of Washington.

I knew Lesle, and I was scared to death of her. For years, she had been a regional ODP coach—one of those frightening people sitting in a chair on the sideline with a clipboard, evaluating every player on the field. Every time I talked to her, I started crying.

One summer, we were at a regional ODP camp in

Laramie, Wyoming. I was selected for the national pool of players, which meant I had to stay for another week. I started to cry—I was just a kid and sick of being in Wyoming. I wanted to go home. Lesle walked over to me. "Hey, Hope," she barked. "The bus is warming up, but it hasn't left yet. Go ahead and get on it if you don't want to be here."

I stopped crying right then and there. Lesle was intimidating.

Oh my God, I thought. *She hates me.*

Her goalkeeping coach at Washington was Amy Allmann, another one of the ODP regional coaches. She was scary and blunt. Of course, it didn't really matter. Lesle and Amy were coaching at Washington, which was about the last place on earth I was planning to go to college. I was going somewhere far from my family.

College coaches could finally contact me directly the summer between my junior and senior years. My phone rang constantly. Even Anson Dorrance, the coach at North Carolina, called. Though I had expected that to be a big moment—after all, he was the most famous soccer coach in the country—it was a letdown. He made me feel that I'd be lucky to go to North Carolina, saying that he usually didn't offer goalkeepers full-ride scholarships. That bothered me; it made me wonder if he respected the position.

Maybe every other player in America wanted to go to North Carolina, but after that phone call, I didn't.

I started to get sick of the recruiters. I just wanted to make a decision and get on with my new life. And then the phone rang again. It was Lesle.

"I thought you guys hated me," I told her.

Back in Seattle, Lesle and Amy had flipped a coin to see who would call me. I was intimidated by them, and now they were intimidated by me. They thought it would be a difficult conversation, because they knew I had no interest in staying in Washington. But they also knew they'd be crazy not to call a kid in their backyard, one they'd been coaching for years. "Well, we thought *you* hated us," Lesle said with a laugh. "But we'd like you to come to take a recruiting visit."

I knew that Cheryl really wanted to go to Washington, which was her father's alma mater. She didn't have any expectations about getting a scholarship to play Division I soccer, but she was a good player and might be able to make the team.

"Okay," I said. "Do you think Cheryl Gies has a chance of making the team?"

Lesle said that she would absolutely have a chance to walk onto the team. That made me happy and I decided I would visit.

I didn't want to go to the University of Washington. But at least I was going to get a cool trip to Seattle.

5

BARE-BRANCHED BUT READY TO BLOOM

I TOOK MY RECRUITING TRIP to the University of Washington on a clear, cold weekend. I had a full schedule: a team breakfast; lunch with Washington's head coach, Lesle Gallimore; a team dinner; and a soccer game to watch that night. My main goal was to have fun and go to a fraternity party or two. I would humor Lesle by showing interest in the soccer team, but I wasn't going to college there.

The Huskies pulled out a close match against USC, winning 3–2. They had a defender playing goalkeeper because their regular keeper had been injured in the previous game and they didn't have a backup. It still didn't matter. There was no way I was going to college there.

I liked the team's determination and the way Lesle coached them. I liked the rowdy support they got from their fans—surprising, considering their relatively low profile in the sport. The enthusiastic Huskies fans reminded me of our boisterous Richland fans. And I liked that Lesle and her assistant, Amy, weren't messing with me—they didn't even promise me a starting spot. They said that maybe I could play forward at times but that I belonged between the posts.

I was the top goalkeeper prospect in the country, one of the top ten recruits overall. But Lesle and Amy were as blunt and honest as they had been back when they had coached me in the Olympic Development Program when I was fourteen and an unknown. They hadn't changed. They weren't fake. I felt I could trust them. I also liked that they had experience on the national level. Lesle had been part of the talent pool in the early years of the U.S. women's national team but had never played in a match. Amy had been a goalkeeper on the national team from 1987 to 1991 and was on the roster in the very first Women's World Cup in 1991, which the United States won. They knew the history of the sport. I didn't.

"Hope," Lesle told me, "I can see you on the gold medal podium for the World Cup."

It was nice to hear that kind of stuff. But really, I had other plans. UW wasn't even considered much of a soccer school. It definitely wasn't a powerhouse like North Carolina. It didn't place players on the national team the way Stanford or Santa Clara did. I knew I could get a full ride at the school of my choice.

On the last day of my UW recruiting trip, I took a walk across campus. I saw students hanging out, enjoying the sunshine. There were people of all different ethnicities, ages, fashion senses, and social strata. I felt comfortable. Not judged. I stopped by the university's music building at the top of the steps leading down into the main quad. The campus spilled out in front of me, redbrick buildings arranged in a rectangle, bare cherry trees that would blossom in clouds of pink the following spring. In the distance, Portage Bay glistened. Beyond it, snowcapped Mount Rainier, the jewel of the Northwest, sat on the horizon like a scoop of ice cream.

I suddenly realized that this was *my* corner of the country, where I belonged. I felt a rush of emotion and a click of recognition so strong that it forced me to sit down hard on the stairs. I wanted to be more than a one-dimensional athlete, a number on a jersey, a prize to be attained by some coach. I wanted more—from my college, from my family, from myself. I was like the cherry trees on the quad—bare-branched but ready to bloom.

There on the steps, my future changed. I could see myself here. I could be a normal college kid, without having to flee from my roots. I could be far enough away to have independence, yet maybe my family could participate in my success and be proud. Maybe my mother and I could build a relationship. My father could even watch me play. I almost started to weep from the force of my sudden conviction. I looked out at Mount Rainier, the smooth white crust covering the volcano below, and knew I should be here.

Grandma would have said God was speaking to me.

By the time I got back to Richland, I knew I was going to be a Husky. But I told Lesle and Amy that I didn't want to announce it yet. I wanted to keep my private business private and be 100 percent sure of my decision, so other coaches were still recruiting me. April kept up the hard sell from Virginia. I knew that April—who had been one of the main assistants to national team head coach Tony DiCicco—could be my ticket into the national team pool. She kept nagging me to take my official visit to Charlottesville, so I finally scheduled it.

Somehow Lesle found out. My phone rang again. "Hope, don't go, don't get on the plane," she said. "You're good enough that no national team coach is going to pick you based on where you go to college. You'll end up getting picked for the national team on merit."

We were on the phone for more than two hours. "If you're just going because of the national team, that's the wrong reason," Lesle said. "That's not fair to Virginia. That's not what the college experience is all about. Don't get on the plane."

I didn't get on the plane. To this day, I've never been to the University of Virginia.

With college still in the murky future, I concentrated on enjoying the present, my senior year of high school. On November 21, we capped our undefeated soccer season by winning the state title, the first-ever championship for Richland High. I scored two goals in the game to bring my four-year total to 109. Within a couple of weeks, I was back on the basketball court, determined to enjoy my last season of competitive hoops. I was key to our man-to-man defense. I loved shutting down the other team's best player, and I was our second-leading scorer.

By the end of senior year, everyone was getting sentimental about going our separate ways and leaving old friends behind.

We graduated in June 1999. My cap and gown were shimmering gold, and I wore a white Hawaiian lei around my neck. When I looked out at the audience,

I saw my father. Terry had made sure he was there—picking him up, getting him cleaned up, putting him in a nice blue shirt, and driving him out to Richland. I was thrilled to see him, but anxiety bubbled up inside of me. I would be going to college in the same city where he lived. Would I see him on a regular basis? Would it be embarrassing? Would my new teammates and friends judge me because of my dad?

We went out to dinner that night with both my family and Cheryl's. It was awkward trying to share my attention between my mom, Glenn, my grandparents, and my dad. I felt divided, trying to please everyone. I wasn't concerned just about my dad. I didn't know how things would be with my mom when I got to Washington. Our relationship was still tense. It was hard to imagine getting to a more relaxed place with her.

That summer was a very cool time to be a soccer player. The Women's World Cup was taking place, and everyone in the country seemed to be talking about women's soccer. A few weeks before my graduation, the U.S. team had played in Portland, and some of my soccer teammates and I made the trip down to see the game. The players signed autographs afterward, and my teammates pushed me toward Briana Scurry. "You should meet the goalkeeper," they said. But the player I really wanted to meet was Michelle Akers.

She was from Washington and was a strong, physical player. She seemed to stand apart from the others, with her bushy hair and powerful game.

I watched every minute of the World Cup games. Cheryl had also gotten into UW, and we watched the games while planning our big move. America's penalty-kick victory in the championship over China was thrilling. Scurry made a save that helped set up the game-winning penalty kick by Brandi Chastain. I was captivated by the effort of Akers, the aging lioness of the team, who gave so much that day that she had to take an IV to rehydrate. I loved her power, her ability to impose her will on opponents. I was still thinking like a forward.

I didn't watch the World Cup games as a fan. I didn't have a poster of Mia Hamm on my wall. I watched like a player—I was planning to someday be on that roster. And a few weeks after the World Cup, I contributed in a small way to what was dubbed the Summer of Soccer.

In late July, the U-18 national team reported for the Pan-American Games in Winnipeg, the first-ever inclusion of women's soccer in the Pan Am Games. Soccer was becoming more than just a distraction from my home life. For the first time, it felt like a full-time job.

I allowed only two goals in the Pan-American

Games, had shutouts in the semifinal and final matches, and my team won the gold medal. It was a great experience: The U.S. men's team was full of up-and-coming young stars such as Landon Donovan and DaMarcus Beasley. Goalkeeper coach Pete Muehler worked with both the men's and women's goalkeepers and had us train together. I trained with Tim Howard and Adin Brown, and Tim and I clicked on the field. After the final, Pete told me that my performance was the best he had seen by any goalkeeper of any gender. It meant a lot for me to hear that from him because he was so well respected. I knew he was passing the word along to the other coaches in U.S. soccer.

I flew through Seattle on my way home to Richland. My dad came and met me at Sea-Tac Airport and waited with me for my connecting flight. He was thrilled to see my medal and stopped total strangers at the airport to tell them what I had accomplished. "My blond Italian goddess," he said over and over. "You're the greatest, Baby Hope. Never sell yourself short."

It was the fall of 1999 and I was finally leaving Richland—and my family—behind. It was time to move to Seattle. My mother drove me over the mountains to help me move into my dorm. We went early because soccer training camp was starting, so there weren't a lot of other students around. I already felt lonely.

We pulled the boxes out of the back of the truck and started hauling them up in the dorm elevator. While my mom was upstairs, I pulled more stuff out of the truck and carried up a load, leaving some of my other possessions on the curb. When I came back down, I saw a man walking away with my small television. I stared after him in shock. "Mom!" I shouted to her as she came out of the dorm. "That man stole my TV."

"Relax," my mother said, and she chased him down the street and got it back.

I felt like a country bumpkin! How was I going to function in a big city without Mom to rescue me? I felt very young and very dumb.

We rushed to unpack because I had to hurry off for the team's preseason physicals. It was time to say good-bye. My mother looked at me, and her eyes welled up with tears. To my surprise, I started crying too. I had never said good-bye to my mother in my whole life. It was my father who was always disappearing. Mom was the one who had always been there. She was the one who had been left with two kids, the one who had to support us and deal with all our problems. She made sure we got to school, that we were fed, that we had the best basketball shoes and a way to get around. She wasn't perfect, but she had tried her hardest. Despite all the harsh words and fights between us, she was the one I knew would never walk out on me. I had been so obsessed with my father's drama that I had taken my mother for granted. Now that I was saying good-bye, I realized I had never needed her more.

"I love you, Hope," she said, hugging me.

"I love you, Mom," I said.

Before my first UW game, my goalkeeper coach, Amy, and I headed out to the field early to warm up. My dad was waiting outside the gate to the stadium. "Hi, Dad," I said, and gave him a hug.

"Hi, Baby Hope," he said. "You look good."

"Thanks," I said awkwardly. "Well, gotta get to work."

I went back to Amy.

"Who's that?" she asked.

"Uh, that's my dad," I said, and left it at that.

When the game started, my dad went to sit high in the uppermost corner of the bleachers, as close to one goal as he could get. When my mother and grandparents arrived, they sat in the "family and friends" section at midfield.

And that's pretty much how it went for my entire UW career—my family split into two sides. My dad would come to games early, often waiting outside the fence when I arrived. He sat at the top of the stands, removed from everyone else. He would watch me intently and sometimes call out, "Let's go, Baby Hope" at a quiet moment. He wanted to make me laugh, but I was determined to keep my serious game face. He wouldn't mingle with the rest of my family—he knew how angry they still were at him. He waited for me after games while I visited with the others. I always felt pulled between the two halves of my family.

A big group from Richland trekked over the mountains for every home game: Mom, Grandma Alice and Grandpa Pete, Aunt Susie, sometimes Marcus. Mary and Dick came to watch Cheryl, who had made the team. Terry drove from Kirkland. My Richland family was unconditionally supportive, but they still hated that I was a goalkeeper. They felt my true talents were on the field. Grandma Alice often wore a T-shirt with my photo on it, covered in buttons with soccer photos of me dating back to grade school. She responded to a fund-raising solicitation from our coaching staff with the following note: "I will only donate a penny for every shutout Hope registers, but I will donate $100 for every goal she scores."

But Lesle and Amy couldn't be bribed. They were thrilled to have a dominant goalkeeper. Still, they remained true to their word. I wasn't handed the starting position. I had to earn it. I split time with a junior, Leslie Weeks. I started twelve games and quickly learned that playing against twenty-one-year-old girls was a huge leap from what I'd been doing. The speed of play was so much faster; there was more brutal contact, and the pressure was intense.

In my twelve games, I made seventy-seven saves, the fourth-highest total in school history. Against BYU, I made thirteen saves, one short of the school regular-season record. But for the first time in a very long time, I learned what it was like to lose. Our team wasn't great. We finished fifth in the Pac-10 Conference that year and didn't make the playoffs. But I never regretted my decision to be at Washington, not once. When my grandparents celebrated their golden fiftieth wedding anniversary, I was able to be there—heading home for a quick trip with Cheryl. And I liked taking my own path, helping to build something new.

That fall was a period of huge adjustments. When I got to UW, I started weight training for the first time. I was living in the dorms and eating cafeteria food. I was no longer the skinny kid who graduated from Richland High. My body was changing. I did what I was told by the trainers. I prided myself in being first in fitness, first in sprints, first in weight training. I was great at drills: I could go up and down, diving for balls a million times and never getting tired. I wanted to work the hardest. But it was a shock to see how quickly my body could change. I was self-conscious of my new muscles. I thought I looked ugly in dresses.

That wasn't the only adjustment. That young, naive feeling I had while I watched a stranger carry off my television never fully went away. At UW, I felt behind everyone else—socially, fashion-wise, even academically. Though I was still a good student, I was more self-conscious in class. I stopped speaking up.

Soon my worries about my dad possibly embarrassing me started to become a reality. Lesle made sure our team did community service, and one week the activity was to feed the homeless at the Union Gospel Mission Men's Shelter in Seattle's Pioneer Square. I'd seen those homeless men lining up outside Union Gospel, in rumpled coats and worn-out shoes.

I was afraid of running into my father. So I just didn't show up. The team got on the bus, and I stayed behind in my dorm and studied.

The next day, Lesle called me aside. "Hey, Hope," she said. "That wasn't an optional activity. Where were you?"

I swallowed hard. "I couldn't go," I said. "I didn't want to see my dad."

Lesle looked surprised. She and Amy had seen my dad at our games, had even exchanged brief hellos.

But they had no idea that he was homeless. After sharing my secret, I let the rest out. I told Lesle the whole story. She listened. She let me talk, without interruption or judgment. "Okay, Hope," she said. "Next time we go to Union Gospel, you don't have to go."

The next time the team went down to Pioneer Square, I went to the library. My teammates thought I was getting a special privilege, that I thought I was too good to feed homeless people.

They didn't know the truth. And Lesle didn't explain.

6

THE '99ERS

I HAD BARELY SETTLED IN at college when I got exciting news: I was going to train with the U.S. Olympic soccer team.

April Heinrichs, who knew me well from having recruited me for Virginia, had been named head coach of the national team in January 2000 after Tony DiCicco retired. Lesle had been right: I was going to be a national team candidate no matter where I went to college. April called me into her first training camp, and I joined the national team players as they prepared for the Algarve Cup, an annual tournament played in Portugal. Though I didn't make the squad that traveled to Portugal, she nevertheless invited me to join the team in Chula Vista, California, where we would live and train for the 2000 Olympics.

I was excited. Less than a year before, during the World Cup, I had hoped to be on the national team. And now I was in the player pool. I withdrew from school for the spring quarter, with Lesle and Amy's support. They knew how important this was.

I was one of the youngest players of the thirty in that camp. I roomed with another young player, Aly Wagner, who was from Santa Clara. Aly was good friends with veteran Tiffeny Milbrett, so I got to know Millie a little. I was full of confidence coming into camp. I didn't idolize the national team players; I just wanted to compete with them. But when I got to Chula Vista, I was hit in the face by what a big deal the team was. Reporters and television crews were hovering. Fans crowded outside the training camp fence. And the skill level of the top players was daunting.

In one of my first practices, Brandi Chastain turned around and barked at me, "That's your ball."

Wow, I thought. *Brandi Chastain is yelling at me.*

Brandi was always yelling. She had made the winning penalty kick at the World Cup. Her teammates called her Hollywood, for her skill at grabbing the spotlight. I liked Brandi, but she intimidated me. She had a lot of opinions and a lot of advice—whether you asked for them or not.

When we were on the road, I roomed with Brandi, but I rarely saw her. She was so busy, rising early, coming back to the room late, locking herself in the bathroom to talk on the phone to her husband while I sat on my bed and studied for my UW independent-study classes.

As much as Brandi talked and yelled on the field and off, Joy Fawcett was the real leader of the defense. She was the smartest defender I ever played behind. She was very even-keeled and didn't try to intimidate the young players, as I felt Brandi did. I loved playing with Joy.

Michelle Akers had helped me get ready for camp. She was also from Washington, and she came out to UW and did drills with me after I got my camp invitation from April. When I arrived at camp, Michelle was my partner in fitness tests. I was honored and in awe of her. I knew that she suffered from chronic fatigue syndrome and that every physical activity was a challenge for her.

Julie Foudy was the team leader off the field. She would meet with the media; she was the team voice. The quietest veteran was Kristine Lilly. The other players were always trying to set her up on dates and give her a makeover—her hair was too big and bushy.

The team's most famous player, Mia Hamm, was also pretty quiet—that is, unless she wanted to get her point across. In one practice game, I was playing with Mia, and I ran out at the top of the box to punt the ball: It went straight up in the air. Mia stopped playing and looked at me. "Do you want me to head the ball? Then you better learn how to drop-kick it."

Oh God, I thought. *Now Mia Hamm is yelling at me.*

I stayed behind after practice that day to work on my dropkick. If I was going to play at that level, I couldn't rely every time on my booming punt—I needed to perfect a lower-trajectory dropkick.

The enduring image of the team was of best friends who would always support one another, but I quickly learned that there were cliques and jealousies.

I just wanted to compete. April had only a few months to figure out her goalkeeper situation. When I joined the team in Chula Vista, I was surprised to see that Briana Scurry—one of the heroines of the '99 team—wasn't in championship form. Her uniform was tight on her. She exhausted easily. She had gained a lot of weight and was suffering from terrible shin splints.

In the aftermath of the World Cup, all the '99 players were awash in new opportunities: They were shooting commercials, endorsing products, making appearances, basking in their new fame. Mia had written a book. Brandi was in a Nike commercial with basketball star Kevin Garnett. Bri made appearances. Everyone agreed that this was great exposure for women's soccer and uncharted territory for women athletes. But Bri had relaxed a little too much. She had, by her own admission, gone home and celebrated. She was confident that she could get her form back quickly, but she couldn't. Diving for balls, running sprints, doing fitness tests—I was kicking her butt. So were the other two relatively inexperienced goalkeepers, Siri Mullinix and Jen Branam. We were outperforming the legendary Briana Scurry.

I was shocked. I didn't understand how you could relax so close to the Olympics and risk missing out on one of the great opportunities in sport. "We have a problem in that we have four good goalkeepers," April told reporters. "We have one with a wealth of experience and three with little experience. . . . Hope knows we don't guarantee playing time. But, at the same time, I have confidence in her."

April was going to cut twelve players before she named the final Olympic roster. She would keep two goalkeepers and make one an alternate. I felt I had a decent shot. I got my first start for the national team on April 5, 2000, against Iceland at Davidson College in North Carolina. The game was closed to the public. In a scheduling quirk, U.S. Soccer wanted back-to-back games with Iceland but felt it could market only one game, so the other was closed. At least I didn't have to deal with the screaming throngs of Mia fans in my debut. A player from North Carolina who was on the Iceland roster lifted a ball right over me that could have been a disaster, but fortunately it bounced wide, right of the goal. That was about the only threat. On offense, our team was ridiculously dominant, scoring eight goals. I had my first appearance for the national team—known in soccer terms as a *cap*—and my first shutout, even if no one saw it.

Then, just one month after my first starting game, I was cut from the national team.

I was scheduled to play against Mexico in the Nike U.S. Women's Cup on Cinco de Mayo. My family drove down from Washington to Portland, Oregon, for the game and attended a family dinner in a banquet room at the hotel. Well-dressed mothers and square-jawed fathers stood in groups and chatted about real estate and the internet boom. My family stood out: Grandma Alice wearing her Hope shirt, my mother tasting every dessert and then asking for a doggie bag. They stood around awkwardly. Few of the other parents came up and introduced themselves. *My family,* I thought, *does not fit in here.* I fought the urge to hide.

For the game against Mexico, 6,500 fans filled the stands at Portland's Civic Stadium. I subbed for Siri in the second half, with a 4–0 lead. We were firmly in control, but in one sequence, Brandi let a ball through the back line, and I had to dive to make a save. Brandi turned around and yelled at me. "Come on, Hope!"

It hadn't been my fault, but I didn't argue. That was my mistake.

After the game, April called me in for a conversation. She wanted to talk about the ball Brandi had missed and our interaction. "That tells me that you're not ready, Hope," she said. "We all knew Brandi made a mistake. Yet you didn't have the courage to call her out and yell back at her. You're not ready to lead this defense."

I knew then that I wasn't going to make the final cut. When the team went to Australia for a pre-Olympic tournament a few weeks later, I wasn't on the traveling roster. I stayed behind in California to train. I was disappointed, but I understood April's decision. I was gifted, competitive, fit, and determined. But I was still learning. I wasn't polished. There was still a lot of work ahead of me.

After the final cut-downs, I went directly to the U-21 team. In Germany, a few days after my nineteenth birthday, we won the Nordic Cup.

Shortly after I was cut from the team, I received a letter from my dad.

> Dear Baby Hope,
>
> It is always so nice to hear from you, you make my day. I miss and love you. Well, Baby Hope, you are the greatest soccer player in the world! Pelé comes second to you. Sorry you didn't make the soccer team—that's their fault. Now you get back to school—you lost a year. . . . You know you can hang with anyone in soccer now. We always knew Baby Hope was the best.
>
> I have an idea, let's have our own soccer team. You be the goalie. Cheryl will be our defender, she has bulldog in her. Marcus, Dave, and I will be strikers—we all have lead in our legs. Your mom will be a defender, she has bulldog, too. She knows how to protect you in more ways than one. Teresa will be the cheerleader, she wouldn't want to get dirty. Jeff can be a midfielder too and Christian has to play. When you are playing striker, Christian will be with you and you can set him up and he will score! Family team—wow.
>
> I hope you don't feel bad, Baby Hope. Just

know you are loved and we all know you are
the greatest. I miss you and don't worry—you
made our dream team in soccer.

Smile and be happy. Take care of your mom.
Tell Marcus I love him.

Baby Hope, my thoughts and prayers are with
you every day and night. I love you so much.

Dad

I laughed at the image my dad created—our family all playing soccer together. I knew he wanted me to remember who my lifelong teammates are.

As the Olympics drew closer, Michelle Akers retired. And April made her choice on the goalkeeper: Siri Mullinix—fresh out of North Carolina—was named the starter over Bri. It was the most controversial decision April had to make, but Bri's lack of fitness made it easier.

On September 28, I was back in Seattle when the United States lost in the Olympic final to Norway on a controversial goal in overtime. A shot bounced off a Norwegian player's arm before she punched it in past Siri. The U.S. women had to settle for the silver medal. Bri admitted she was bitter over being benched.

Back at school, I felt like an outsider. While I'd been off pursuing my soccer dreams, college had gone on without me. My teammates had gotten closer to one another, bonding in the second half of freshman year. It seemed that a new social order had formed, and everyone knew about it except me. Even Cheryl—now tight with our teammates Megan and Suz—had a personal life that didn't include me. It hurt. I think some of the awkwardness probably stemmed from jealousy. I knew other girls thought I was arrogant because of my national team experience. I couldn't even grab a clean T-shirt out of my drawer without hearing people talking about me behind my back. "Oh my God, she has to wear her national team gear all the time. She thinks she's so great."

Wow, I thought. *Be careful what you wish for. Once you reach a certain level, everything you do will be critiqued.*

I didn't feel like a different person. Through my experience with the national team, I'd been exposed to a lot. I felt I'd grown up. But when I got back to school, I felt that everyone else had moved on without me. Even Cheryl. That was the most painful part. We were still like sisters—we always had been and always would be. Lesle and Amy still relied on Cheryl to find out what was going on with me in my personal life, but she had branched out and formed new relationships. I had new friends, too, like my teammate Malia Arrant, who was two years ahead of me. But I was hurt by the distance between me and Cheryl. She wouldn't tell me about certain things—like this one party she'd been to that I had missed. I know she was trying to protect my feelings, but it stung, because Cheryl was the one person I could always count on to tell me the truth.

I think Cheryl saw that soccer was becoming a career for me, and in many ways it was. I was working hard at it, and I was getting paid for my work. I bought a Chevy Blazer, and now I could afford to go on spring break trips or snowboarding weekends like other UW kids. I felt rich, thanks to soccer.

Maybe Cheryl was right: I was more businesslike. I didn't goof around and gossip as much as some of my teammates. I felt at times that they didn't take soccer as seriously as I did, didn't view it as a potential career. Despite all that, we were functioning well as a team on the field. I started all twenty-one games for UW my sophomore year and set a school record for fewest goals allowed in a season. We won eighteen games and our first-ever Pac-10 championship and made it all the way to the Sweet Sixteen of the NCAA tournament. Lesle was named the Pac-10 Coach of the Year.

Though I didn't know where my father was living, he was still a fixture in the stands. There even seemed to be a slight thawing in the relationship between the two sides of my family. Sometimes my mother would climb to the top of the stands and give him peace offerings of cookies or a cup of cocoa. She knew he was hungry. And she understood how important it was for me to have him there, supporting me. She knew that I needed my father in my life.

Once I got my own car, I gave him rides. He usually asked me to just drop him off by the side of the highway, near a freeway exit west of UW. But eventually he let me see the small tent that he lived in, deep in the woods. I learned that I shouldn't have worried about running into him at the Union Gospel Mission Men's Shelter—he avoided the large homeless population downtown that filled the shelters and lined up outside the soup kitchens. He said he preferred being out in the woods alone. Sometimes, after my games, I bought macaroni and cheese or picked up hero sandwiches and sat in a park with him, eating and talking about sports. I was finding I really enjoyed his company. I knew that I hated being judged by others, so I did my best not to judge him but simply appreciate him for who he was.

My dad doted on me and wanted to hear about everything in my life—the national team, UW, my Husky teammates. In many ways we had a richer, more loving relationship than I had with my mother or brother. I became dependent on his advice and encouragement. The man who had been absent for so much of my life was now someone I relied on. For better or worse, he was family, and I was focusing on the "for better" part.

In December, I rejoined the national team. We played Mexico in a game in Texas, and this time I subbed in the second half for Siri. I let in two goals, including one memorably bad one—I tried to clear a ball and miskicked it. I was too far out of the goal to get back to make the save, and Mexico took a 2–1 lead. Fortunately, Cindy Parlow scored twice later in the game to get us the win, but after the game I was still feeling a little shaky.

But April hadn't given up on me. In January she named me to the traveling roster of a young team she was taking to China, for a two-game series with our longtime rivals. After my mishap against Mexico, I was determined to make a good impression. I was enjoying the trip. I felt that I got to know the veterans who were on the team, like Christie Pearce (everyone called her "Pearcie") and Lorrie Fair. I was making some inroads and beginning to find a comfort level.

Early in the trip, April called me into her hotel room and told me to have a seat. I was very nervous. Was she going to tell me, again, that I wasn't ready to start? "Hope," she said. "I hear something is wrong with your father."

My stomach flipped and my heart started pounding. I felt faint. I stood up to head toward the door and then sat back down—not wanting to be rude to April but desperate to get away from her and call my mom. Did she mean my dad or my stepfather, Glenn? Had there been an accident?

"Your father," April said, "has been accused of murder."

7

"I SHOULD HAVE DIED A LONG TIME AGO"

THE DAY BEFORE I LEFT for China, a grisly murder made headlines in Seattle. A forty-year-old real estate agent named Mike Emert was found dead in an upscale home for sale in Woodinville, an area northeast of the city. By nightfall, police had identified my father as a "person of interest" and had taken him into custody for questioning.

I didn't know it, but the night before our team left town, a detective knocked on Lesle's door and asked for my address. He told her my father was implicated in a murder case. Lesle was shocked—she had gotten to know my dad a little, and she couldn't believe the accusation, but her main concern was for me; she stalled the detective, telling him I was out of the country, even though I wasn't leaving until the next morning. Police called my mother's home in Richland. They tracked down Marcus. They were on the hunt for any information they could find.

Of all the members of our family, I had had the most regular contact with my father, but I was six thousand miles away. Lesle and Amy were worried that either the police or the media would track me down in China, or that I would randomly find out—one of my teammates had a sister who was a Seattle cop. My coaches and family were eager to protect me as much as possible. Lesle called the team's sports psychologist, who was with us in China, and explained the situation.

"Don't tell Hope," Lesle told her. "She doesn't need to know about this until she gets home. We're trying to keep it quiet on campus. But she might find out somehow, and I want you to be aware."

Things didn't go exactly as planned. The psychologist told April, who just blurted out the bombshell: "Hope, your father has been accused of murder."

I was frantic. I called my mom and Marcus, trying to make sense of the whole thing. Was my father in custody? Had anyone seen him? Nobody knew where he was.

Back in my room, I huddled in front of a computer in my hotel in China and read the lead of the story in the *Seattle Post-Intelligencer*.

He admits to a troubled past . . . But he insists he's not a killer.

Nonetheless, authorities investigating the slaying of Eastside Realtor Mike Emert are now focusing on Jeffrey John Solo—the mysterious man with a limp whom they consider a "person of interest" in the case.

Jeffrey John Solo. The man I knew as Dad. His picture was on the paper's front page. The story said my father had come to the *Seattle Post-Intelligencer* building to tell his side of the story. Days earlier, he had been taken into custody, had been given a polygraph test, had hair and blood samples taken, and then had been released. But he remained a "person of interest."

He matched the description of the suspect in a few key ways: He walked with a limp, carried a cane, and had a thick New York accent.

But it was the final lines of the story that broke my heart.

He says he came forward to protect the reputation of another daughter, who lives in Seattle.

"I don't care about myself or what happens to me. I should have died a long time ago," he said. "But my daughter, I don't want her to get hurt. That's why I'm telling my story. I didn't do this."

Alone in China, I stared at the computer screen and wept.

We still had four days left on our trip, and I was getting another chance in goal. But it was hard to focus on soccer with all the drama swirling around me. Where was my father? Was he safe?

Yet I played well. As a young player, I had learned to shut out the many crises in my personal life whenever I stepped on the soccer field. That served me well in China. I got my chance against the Chinese national team in Hangzhou, where thirty thousand fans showed up to watch the competition.

It was freezing when we walked onto the pitch. We took an early lead, but China tied us, 1–1, on a free kick that bent over our line and into the upper left corner of the goal. Overall, I had an excellent game. In the second half, I made a few diving saves. The ball got through our back line several times, but I didn't give up another goal. The game ended in a draw.

When we left China the next day, I didn't know what would greet me at the airport. Would I be ambushed by reporters and photographers? The sensational story continued to make headlines. All the reports noted that Jeffrey John Solo had a nineteen-year-old daughter in Seattle. Though none identified me by name, it wouldn't take Sherlock Holmes to figure that the nineteen-year-old daughter from Richland with the same memorable last name, sometimes described as a "star athlete," was UW's goalkeeper.

Fortunately, Lesle had been doing damage control the entire time I'd been gone. She enlisted our sports information director to control the story on the UW end. She called our team together and warned that if anyone spoke to the media, they would be suspended. Lesle and Amy protected me. Their support during this family nightmare made me even more loyal to them and prouder that I had chosen UW.

Cheryl picked me up at the airport. There were no cameras or reporters.

"Let's go find your dad," she said.

The stories I had read said he'd been staying at a friend's apartment, but the friend had become upset by police harassment and had kicked him out. We drove all around Seattle, but he was nowhere to be found. I walked through parks in the rain, looking for him.

After days of frantic worry, my father called. We decided to meet at REI, the large outdoor equipment store in downtown Seattle. When I saw him waiting for me outside the store, I ran into his arms. It was such a relief to see him, to see that he was all right. "Baby Hope, you know I didn't do this," he said.

"Of course I know that," I said.

He told me the police had questioned him for hours, browbeating him in an attempt to get a confession. But he told me he had stood his ground, telling them over and over, "I didn't do it." He said the harsh treatment might have broken him if he had been younger, that he could now understand how people confess to crimes they didn't commit. But as he liked to remind me, he was "a tough son of a gun."

I had never seen my father so upset. He felt he was being framed. He didn't understand why the police were hounding him. He had an alibi—he had been at a doctor's appointment at the VA hospital the day the murder was committed. He had taken a lie detector test and was sure he had passed. But the police were still harassing him.

As my father told me of his ordeal, he broke down

in tears. "You know, Baby Hope, I did a lot of bad things in my life," he said. "Maybe this is payback for all of that."

He had gone to the *Seattle Post-Intelligencer* out of fear that I would be linked to the news story and that my reputation would be harmed. He agreed to an exclusive interview in exchange for withholding my name.

"I just want to make sure you're protected," he told me.

In the spring of 2001, April named me to the national team squad that traveled to Europe and then on to the Algarve Cup in Portugal. She was taking a very young team: All the national team veterans were getting ready for the inaugural season of the WUSA, the professional league they had founded. So our traveling roster was full of college players, including a few I had never heard of. Our average age was nineteen. Despite the hodgepodge of talent, it was fun to be with players of my own generation—and not excluded by the veterans. But it felt a little too comfortable.

It was the worst U.S. performance ever in the prestigious Portuguese tournament. We lost three games, including the two I started, to teams that had brought their full senior rosters. In a 3–0 loss to Canada, their veteran star, Charmaine Hooper, chipped a ball over me in the first half. And a new Canadian player named Christine Sinclair scored off a corner kick: It was the first battle of many between us. Sweden beat us, 2–0, in my second start.

While I was traveling, I heard that my father had been officially cleared in the Emert murder case. Sort of. A story in the *Seattle Post-Intelligencer* made it clear the police still had doubts about him.

> *"We don't believe that he was part and parcel to the homicide," King County Sheriff's Office spokesman John Urquhart said yesterday. "We're still trying to figure out what, if any, connections to the crime Mr. Solo may have."*
>
> *Authorities have not ruled out the possibility that Emert's killer may have set Solo up to look like the killer, Urquhart said, or that Solo was somehow involved in another way.*

My father had taken and passed two polygraph tests, and his alibi was solid: A physician at the VA Hospital confirmed that he had seen my father that day.

When I returned to Seattle, I could tell that my father was frustrated. He didn't feel his name was fully cleared. He was still being harassed by police, banned by shopkeepers. The taint of the murder accusation lingered, and would for years. Marcus and I stood by him.

I knew that others in my family doubted whether my father was truly innocent.

For a long time, I would hear other family members speculate about my father's role in the murder. Those doubts infuriated me. I knew he was innocent.

Meanwhile, the Emert murder remained unsolved. There wasn't any real closure for his widow and daughter. Or for my father.

Even so, things started looking up for him around this time. The VA Hospital had not only provided an alibi for my father, but it also threw him a lifeline. Friends my dad made there helped secure him low-income housing at Hilltop House, an affordable complex for the elderly in downtown Seattle. My father had a roof. He had food.

After years on the street, he had a place to call home.

8

AN ARM LIKE FRANKENSTEIN

AFTER A SLOW START, I was getting the hang of college life.

I dated a few different guys, but then I met Adrian. A grown-up by my standards and seemingly worldly, he was twenty-five years old and managing nightclubs; he had played soccer in community college and didn't care one way or the other about my soccer career. He made it clear that he'd rather watch water boil than women's soccer. I took that as a challenge.

Adrian liked to do the same stuff I did: shoot hoops or go snowboarding or just hang out. He was easy to be with, and pretty soon I was spending most of my free time with him. I still dated other guys, and he dated plenty of women, but when we were together, it felt special. And I needed a friend. There was a widening gap in my life as Cheryl and I grew apart. Malia had graduated, and every time I came back from a stint with the national team, I felt pushed further out of the college circle. I was living a dual existence with my college and national teams, pulled between two sets of women who often seemed less like friends than work colleagues. I wanted a friend I could count on—who wouldn't feel our friendship had suffered because I was traveling. Someone I could pick back up with where I had left off, without a lot of drama.

Adrian made me comfortable. He didn't pass judgment—not on my family or my background or my father. He had his own rocky past and complicated family matters. He'd grown up in West Seattle, also from a broken home. Like me, he was resilient.

For a long, long time Adrian and I insisted—to outsiders and to each other—that we were just friends.

In 2001, the summer before my junior year of college, I was named to the preseason list of candidates for the Hermann Trophy, the award given to the nation's outstanding collegiate soccer player. Just making the list was an honor—goalkeepers were rarely considered for the award. Lesle made sure that everyone—on our team, at UW, and on the outside—knew that the nomination was a testament to how important I was to the Huskies.

The season before, UW had won its first-ever Pac-10 Conference championship. Eight of our games had been decided by one goal, and five of those were shutouts. We had great senior leadership in Malia Arrant, Theresa Wagner, and Tami Bennett. I looked up to those upperclassmen and followed their lead. I may have stopped a lot of shots, but it was a collaborative effort. We finished the season ranked number three in the nation. UW soccer was on the map, and I had helped put it there. That was a great feeling.

Also on the Hermann Trophy list was my good friend Aly Wagner and a relatively unknown player named Abby Wambach from the University of Florida. Abby was a year older than me but hadn't yet been in the national team pool. She was a raw, powerful player whose first significant national team play was in the Nordic Cup in 2001. Our U-21 coach, Jerry Smith, Brandi Chastain's husband, picked her. I didn't know much about Abby before training camp for the Nordic Cup, where we were roommates. She was rough around the edges but had great athleticism. At the Nordic Cup, she made an instant impact, scoring three goals but also drawing two yellow cards, which forced her to sit out our championship victory over Sweden. That was Abby in a nutshell: great ability combined with a power and force rarely seen in women's soccer. She sometimes ran right through opponents and intimidated them with her strength.

That September, Abby and I were among April's call-ups for the Nike Cup training camp. The team was a blend of veterans, who had just finished their inaugural WUSA season, and young players. Five of us were interrupting our college seasons to play for the national team: a sign that the national team was serious about targeting the next generation of players and giving us meaningful playing time. I felt a bond with those other collegiate players who were being pulled out of school to play for the national team. Unlike my UW teammates, they lived the same dual life I did and understood the aspects of college life that we gave up—the football games and parties and hanging out on the weekends. Like me, they were packing up textbooks along with their cleats, saying good-bye to boyfriends and best friends, again and again. For us, soccer wasn't just a fun pastime. It was our job.

I'd been in camp a few weeks when I tore my right groin in training. I flew home immediately to start my rehabilitation. I'd already missed two UW games and wanted to be ready to play for the Huskies for the rest of my junior year. Doctors told me the injury would keep me out for three weeks, but I didn't miss a game. It was the first significant injury I had suffered during college, the first time I had needed serious pain medication. But I didn't want to miss any more UW games. I taped up the injury and played out the rest of the season, even though I was unable to kick with my right foot. The good news was that I found out I had a pretty decent left foot.

Despite my limited mobility, I made sixty-eight saves and helped the Huskies to a 12–4–1 record, second place in our conference. We were a good team, with a talented freshman class and more top recruits in the pipeline. One of our new players was Tina Frimpong, another Washington high school sensation.

Our team lost in the second round of the NCAA tournament that year, bounced yet again by Christine Sinclair and the University of Portland. I didn't win the Hermann Trophy, but I got a consolation prize: I was named the Pac-10 Player of the Year, the first Washington player to receive the award and the first-ever goalkeeper.

In February of my junior year, the U-21 national team was in Chihuahua, Mexico, playing against

Mexico's senior team. Their star, Maribel Dominguez, took a free kick with ten minutes to play in a scoreless game. She sailed the ball toward the far post, and as I dove to block it, I hit the post and felt myself get caught on something. As the ball went into the net, my body lurched in a circle, still attached to the pole, and I thudded to the ground.

My teammates were shouting, "Get up, Hope! Get up!" They were running into the goal to get the ball—eager to tie the game—while I lay motionless, unable to move. Something was terribly wrong. I looked down to make sure my arm was still there, because I couldn't feel it—was it still dangling from the post? The arm was there and I didn't see anything wrong. There wasn't any blood. There was no tear in the jersey. When I lifted up my jersey sleeve I gasped. A hole gaped in my forearm; the muscle and tendons were hanging out. I could see the yellow of the fat, the white of my bone. My forearm had gotten caught on a hook on the inside of the goalpost and had been ripped wide open. I panicked, fearing that the insides of my arm were going to fall out. I took my filthy goalkeeper glove and covered the hole and sprinted off the field, with my defender, Natalie Spilger, running along beside me, screaming. On the sideline, my goalkeeper coach took one look at my arm and had to sit down. I turned paper white and went into shock.

Our team doctor went with me to a nearby hospital, where she insisted that she was in charge. She made sure everything was disinfected, and then stitched up the jagged gash. It was hideous—my arm looked like a Frankenstein body part, connected to the rest of me by giant stitches.

That night in my hotel room, I couldn't sleep. My forearm was throbbing with pain, the sutures oozing. I couldn't feel my fingers and was certain I had nerve damage. Would I ever be able to use my arm again? I started to panic. It was hard to breathe. What if my career was over? What would I do with my life? Could a rusty hook on a Mexican goalpost end all that? If I couldn't play, who was I?

I slid out of bed, down to the cool tile floor, and prayed. After a few moments, I felt a sense of calm come over me.

I breathed in the earthy smell of the clay tile. "Hope," I said loud enough to wake up my roommate, "you're going to be okay."

Thankfully, I didn't have to give up soccer. My arm healed and, aside from a nasty purple scar, was as good as new. In 2002, during my last full year at UW, I juggled international trips to Portugal for the Algarve Cup and to Iceland for another Nordic Cup championship. I crammed through my classes to make sure I would graduate on time. And I earned money by coaching youth goalkeepers. Whenever I could, I went to see my dad.

Lesle believed our team would become stronger by being tested in tough nonconference games. We usually played powerhouses like Portland and Santa Clara. In my senior year, though, she outdid herself: She scheduled us in the Carolina Classic tournament in September, playing Duke and North Carolina. Those were two of the top teams in the country, but we were making our mark nationally: ranked number eleven to start the season. We lost both Carolina Classic games.

I missed them both because I was with the national team for a game against Scotland in Columbus, Ohio. I got the start, and was replaced by Bri in the second half. Abby didn't start but came off the bench to score a hat trick (three goals in one game)—probably the moment she became indispensable to the national team.

I didn't know it, but that was the last game I would play for the national team for the next two and a half years. April was still encouraging and supportive, but Bri had regained her form and, having learned tho hard way, was determined not to let go of the starting spot again.

Back at UW, I wanted to make the most of my senior year.

On the field, our team was struggling. Our ambitious schedule hurt us: We lost eight games, seven to ranked opponents. We had a lot of talent, but everyone seemed to be pointing fingers rather than scoring goals. I was a captain, but I felt ineffective. I had one foot in the national team camp and couldn't give UW my complete attention. And I was frustrated by what I saw. At one team meeting, a freshman started to argue with Lesle about a formation she was implementing. I stood up. "This isn't high school," I shouted. "Why don't you listen to someone who knows about the game?"

I stormed out. It wasn't an appropriate reaction for a senior captain, but I felt having a know-it-all freshman take over the meeting was bad. When I had been a younger player, I looked up to our juniors and seniors. But now our team seemed irreparably broken. When we lost to UCLA in our final home weekend, I was disappointed. My senior season hadn't gone as I had hoped. No happy ending.

Lesle gave me a hug after the game. "I'm glad you have Adrian," she said. "I know you need someone to lean on away from the team."

When selections were made for the NCAA postseason tournament, UW was left out. The selection committee didn't consider our strength of schedule. They just saw all the losses. Portland, led by Christine

Sinclair, won the national championship. I ended my career at UW with every school goalkeeper record, including my 18 shutouts, 325 saves, and a goals-against average of 1.02. But statistics never mattered to me. The important thing was that—finally—I had learned to become a goalkeeper.

Not long after I first put on the purple UW jersey—choosing number 18 so that I could keep my options with a number a field player would wear—my goalkeeper coach, Amy, handed me a note that said, "A goalkeeper cannot win a game. She can only save it." I made those words my computer screen saver and read them every day.

In high school, I had been the forward who won games. It was a huge mental adjustment to learn that my job was to save games. To be patient in goal. To anticipate what was needed. Amy taught me the nuances of being a goalkeeper. Before, I would stand in goal, the ball would come toward me, and I'd use my athletic ability to make the save. But thanks to Amy's tutelage and my time with the national team, I was becoming a much better tactical goalkeeper. I learned how to read my opponents' runs toward goal, how to position my defenders, how to see the angles. I learned when to come off my line and when to stay back, how to start a counterattack, how to anticipate and predict what was happening in front of me.

Amy—all five feet four of her—had to know the game to compete as a goalkeeper on the national team. She taught me that side and how to incorporate it with my athleticism. The intellectual side also made goalkeeping so much more interesting. It wasn't just ninety minutes of waiting for my defense to make a mistake. It was ninety minutes of tactics and strategy.

It had taken eight years, but I was finally a real goalkeeper.

In February of my senior year, Adrian and I flew to Atlanta for the WUSA draft. The professional league was starting its third season, and I was among the top players in the country, invited to attend the draft in person. I had already chosen an agent, Richard Motzkin. And I had a deal in the works with Nike.

My name was called on the fourth pick—I was going to play for the Philadelphia Charge. Philadelphia. I would have to move to the other side of the country. Away from my family, and away from Adrian.

I was now a professional soccer player. That there was a professional league for women seemed like a natural development in a world where the 1999 Women's World Cup had sold out football stadiums, where fans crushed against fences to see Mia Hamm, where girls like me had been rewarded all our lives for working hard and playing well. It seemed like a natural step—but for me it was still a scary one. "Oh my God, Adrian, I have to move to Philadelphia," I said. "I'm really going to miss you."

"Do you want me to come with you?" he said.

I thought he was kidding. "Would you really?" We were just friends, right? Really good friends.

He said, "When you love someone as much as I love you, it's not even a question of whether I'll come."

My breath caught in my chest. It was the first time he'd said he loved me.

I went back to Seattle and finished my classes, and then I was done with school. I had completed my communications degree. I went into the athletic building to say good-bye to Lesle and Amy and felt a wave of emotion. Going to UW was the best decision I ever made. If I had followed my original vow and gone as far away from home as possible, I might never have gotten to know my father, never improved my relationship with my mother, never learned as much about goalkeeping, never had coaches who would be role models and lifelong friends.

It was only fitting that I missed one more thing at UW because of soccer: my graduation ceremony. While my classmates donned caps and gowns, I was riding the bench for the Philadelphia Charge.

9

MADE IN THE WUSA

THE BALL CAROMED OFF THE crossbar, and Abby Wambach pounced on it, sending a rocket into the corner of the net. She was on fire; it was her third goal against us, but I couldn't do anything but watch, because I wasn't in the game. I was sitting on the bench while the Washington Freedom, a team that starred Abby and Mia Hamm, manhandled my Philadelphia Charge.

Professional soccer wasn't turning out to be what I expected. The launch of the Women's United Soccer Association in 2001—the first professional soccer league for women—seemed to me like a natural evolution, not a revolution. Women's sports were growing stronger every year. Why shouldn't we have our own league?

When Philadelphia drafted me, I felt I had

arrived—a professional athlete, in the same category as Shaq or A-Rod. But by early May, I was learning the hard truth women's professional soccer wasn't anything like the NBA or Major League Baseball. I had joined a league fighting desperately to stay alive. Corporate sponsorships weren't panning out, crowds were nowhere near projections, and television ratings were low. The league was in financial trouble. I had barely unpacked before I was asked to take a pay cut, dropping my salary from $35,000 to $30,000.

I felt alone and homesick for the first time. After a lot of discussion, Adrian hadn't come with me. He had too many business projects in Seattle, and we were both worried about his moving to Philadelphia just to be with me. I also didn't have Cheryl, or Lesle, or Amy.

But the most unsettling thing was that since the Philadelphia Charge didn't have a goalkeeping coach, the starting goalie, Melissa Moore, effectively took on the role. During practices, the coaches would send us off to the side to work together. How, I wondered, would anyone know if I beat her out? I couldn't even compete for the job. I knew she had seniority, but I just wanted a fair shot.

So I sat on the bench and watched as we lost game after game. Finally, as the season dragged on, I decided to offer my opinion during one of our film sessions. "You were out of position," I said to Melissa, then turned to coach Mark Krikorian. "Maybe we should get a goalkeeper coach to break down the film."

Mark didn't like that. Melissa was his protégée. He called Amy. "What's the deal with this kid?" he said.

"What do you mean? She's awesome. She's a hard worker. She wants to prove herself."

"Is she coachable?" Mark said. "She seems awfully immature."

Maybe I was. Some of my teammates, like Heather Mitts, were surprised that I had spoken up in the film room. Mark, some teammates warned me, didn't want to hear from players who disagreed with him.

I was getting worried about my career. I knew Mark's refusal to play me was hurting my chances for the national team, and the Women's World Cup was coming up in September 2003—the first World Cup since the epic 1999 tournament—and it was back on U.S. soil. Every player in the national team pool was training hard with the World Cup in mind. China had originally been slated to host the event, but the SARS epidemic of early 2003 caused a panic about travel to Asia. In May, the Fédération Internationale de Football Association decided to move the World Cup to the United States with just four months' notice. The rationale was that the United States

Soccer Federation could handle last-minute planning and that the tournament might bolster the struggling WUSA. China was awarded the rights to the 2007 World Cup.

Portland, which would serve as one of the host cities, was just three hours south of my hometown. For three years, I had been in and out of the national team pool, and I felt I had a chance to make the roster this time. But I needed to play. In every Charge match, I saw national team players starting for the opposition. Bri was starting for Atlanta. Siri was starting for the Washington Freedom and would ultimately lead them to the league championship. That was what the WUSA was supposed to be about: developing players with high-level regular competition. But I was stuck watching someone else's mistakes on video.

April actually lobbied Mark to get me some playing time, but he stuck with Melissa as the hot, muggy Philadelphia summer dragged on. I was miserable. Finally, after a 3–1 loss on July 26 to Carolina, the Charge was officially eliminated from playoff contention. We had been at the bottom of the league all season and had gone 0–5 in July. With nothing to lose, Mark decided to play me.

I started the final three games of the season. Against Atlanta, I earned my first professional shutout in a 3–0 win. Against Washington, I shut out the eventual champions, helping to hold Abby and Mia scoreless. In the season finale at Carolina, we tied 1–1, though we might have won if we had converted a late-game penalty kick. Mark had started playing me too late for my World Cup chances, but I finished the season with three wins and a tie and a little more confidence.

It had been a rough rookie season. I vowed to myself that my second season in the WUSA would be better.

Thirty-seven days after I played my last game for the Philadelphia Charge, the WUSA folded. Though I'd known the league was struggling, I was shocked.

Back in Seattle, I sat on the couch and contemplated my future. How was I going to support myself? I was twenty-two and had been told for years that I had potential, potential, potential. But did the national team even have a spot for me? I felt I was going backward. It was 2003, and I wasn't any further along than I had been in 2000. I hadn't played in a national team game for more than a year. What was I going to do?

I wasn't the only one worrying. The vibe for the '03 World Cup was nothing like it had been in '99. The crowds were smaller and less enthusiastic—the roar in '99 had turned into a whisper.

On October 5, the United States lost 3–0 to Germany

in a semifinal game in Portland. There wouldn't be any repeat championship. I sat in the stands with Adrian, watching my teammates openly weep on the field. My good friend Cat fell to the ground and lay there sobbing until a veteran came over and pulled her to her feet. It was a depressing end to a sad summer for women's soccer.

While I figured out what to do with my life, I kept coaching kids. My friend Malia had become the coaching director of one of the biggest clubs in Seattle, and she hired me as a goalkeeper coach and connected me with parents looking for private training. I found the work fulfilling and felt that I connected with the kids.

I spent a lot of time with my father during those months, curling up on his couch to nap between coaching gigs. I felt I could tell him anything—what I was thinking, how I was feeling. We talked about sports, about the future. Our relationship blossomed.

Adrian and I enjoyed living in West Seattle, near Alki Beach Park. We played beach volleyball and prowled our neighborhood cafés. As always, our time together was special, but we kept it casual. I was just staying at his apartment: no serious commitment. That's what we said, but we liked living together.

Around the holidays, my agent called. A First Division Swedish team, Kopparbergs/Göteborg, in southern Sweden, had offered me a contract. *Why not?* I thought. It sounded like an adventure, a chance to make some money, and a way to prove to April and national team goalkeeper coach Phil Wheddon that I was determined to get better. I needed game action, and I would get it in Sweden.

In February, I flew to Göteborg and then headed directly to the Canary Islands for training camp, where I met my new teammates. I was the only American on the team. Playing in Sweden changed my life. Without college obligations or family demands or the chase for the national team carrot, I rediscovered my love for the game. I wasn't trying to please anyone or move up a ladder or prove anything to April. I relaxed and had fun.

And I could tell I was getting better on the field. The pace of the game was faster than in the WUSA; I had to make quicker decisions and take charge. Our team was playing well, and I was considered one of the top goalkeepers in a pretty good league.

I grew up a lot in Sweden, taking long walks in the woods outside of town with my closest friend, midfielder Sofia Palmqvist, who was a deep thinker. We were both in our twenties and trying to figure out life. We talked about our dreams. We played Dance Dance Revolution in my apartment and went dancing in Göteborg. I also spent a lot of time alone, reading books like Dan Millman's *Way of the Peaceful Warrior*, about an athlete on a spiritual journey. I started a journal. I began to read the Bible. I wanted to find my center, to expand my heart and mind.

I called my dad and sent him postcards, and I called my mother almost every day. Now that I was far away from my family, I appreciated their support and love even more.

I had to move five thousand miles away to fully appreciate that.

In late May 2004, I left my Swedish team and flew back to the United States for the Olympic residency camp in Southern California. April was finalizing her roster for the Athens Olympics, and—except for a few games with the Charge—she hadn't seen me play since September 2002. I had few expectations about making the Athens roster. I was just happy with my progress in Sweden, and I wasn't nervous about impressing the national team coaches. Everyone could tell that something about me had changed. On the field, I felt looser and more confident. I had an excellent two weeks of training and then returned to Sweden.

When the Athens roster was named in late June, the two goalkeepers on the team were Bri and Kristin Luckenbill. Luckenbill was a Dartmouth graduate who had started for three years for the Carolina

WUSA team but hadn't played on the national level. Her emergence left me little hope of being named an alternate—I assumed that that final slot on the team would go to an experienced goalkeeper like Siri. But in early July—a few games before my Swedish team went on an extended break for the Olympics—April and Phil called me. "Hope, we want you to be our alternate," Phil said. "We can see how much you've grown in Sweden. Because you've been playing competitive games, we think you'd be better prepared than the goalkeepers who have only been able to train."

My first reaction was to jump up and down. My second was to immediately shoot off an email to Lesle and Amy.

> I'm writing to tell you guys that I'm going to Greece as the third goalkeeper. Although I want to be the first! :) I feel very rewarded, and I feel a step closer to my dreams. It's a great feeling and I couldn't wait to tell you since you two have been through it all with me, right there by my side. It's taken several years, but slowly, it's all coming together, and I want to thank you for all your support and for truly believing in me. Washington, and all it had to offer, really set me straight!!! You

guys are the best, and forever in my heart
and mind! I love you. Hope.

In early August, I had to meet the national team on Crete for training. I was always with the team on the field, but because I was an alternate, I was separated from them the rest of the time. I couldn't even get into the team meals. Once again, I felt like an outsider.

In Athens, I fell in love with the Olympics. As a fan, I saw the Olympic spirit, the pride of the Greeks, the enthusiasm in the stands, the hugeness of the event. The Olympics were different from other sporting events; their meaning hadn't been damaged by all the modern commercialism and hype. Maybe being in Greece, the birthplace of the Games, helped me understand that there was something profound about this gathering of the world's countries. I was determined to be a full participant the next time around.

My teammates rode a wave of emotion into the final. The gold-medal game against Brazil was the last competition for the core of the '99 team. Mia Hamm, Julie Foudy, and Joy Fawcett had announced that they would retire after the Games. No one was sure what the future held for Brandi Chastain or Kristine Lilly or Bri. They didn't say they were retiring, but an era was definitely ending.

For much of the gold-medal game, there was a sense that the world of soccer was undergoing a changing of the guard. Brazil—led by its skilled forward Marta—completely outplayed our team. I sat in the stands with Adrian, watching nervously. Brazil had scoring chance after scoring chance, hitting the post twice with potential game winners late in regulation. After ninety minutes, the game was tied 1–1. But in the twenty-second minute of overtime, Abby headed a corner kick in for the winning goal. Our team was able to kill the clock and finally celebrate.

I knew a new era was beginning for U.S. soccer—one that would include me.

After finishing out my Swedish season, I returned to Seattle. When I got back, Adrian and I felt a distance between us. We broke up soon after my homecoming, and I loaded up my car with all my belongings and moved out of our shared apartment. My heart was broken. I didn't have anywhere to live. My beloved Seattle felt like a trap. I needed to leave.

Fortunately, my agent called with another contract offer in Lyon, France, playing for Olympique Lyonnais. In late December, I boarded a plane.

Several weeks later, as I was adjusting to life in Lyon, I got word from across the Atlantic of a huge national team shakeup. April had resigned as head coach.

One morning my phone rang. "Hi, Hope," said the voice on the other end. "This is Greg Ryan."

10

BAA, BAA, BLACK SHEEP

IF I HAD MADE A list of all the people I thought might coach the national team, Greg Ryan would probably have been dead last. Greg had been April's unremarkable assistant coach. He mostly faded into the background, rarely talking and never taking charge at practice. If he had any leadership skills, we never saw them. We figured he got the job simply because he was a friend of April's. I don't think any of the national team players really felt they knew him. But now, in February 2005, he was on the other end of the phone, telling me that he was the interim national team coach. And that I was on his roster for the upcoming Algarve Cup in Portugal.

I felt bad for April. She had always been my supporter—all the way back to when I was first in the Olympic Development Program as a kid in Richland. She gave me my first break on the national team and was always straightforward and honest about what I needed to do to improve.

In the press, her departure was portrayed as a resignation, but I knew she had been forced out by the veteran players. I'd heard their grumblings—they'd been lobbying to get rid of her for years, unhappy with her soccer tactics, her awkward communication skills, and her leadership style.

Now Greg Ryan was the head coach. And I wasn't the only one getting a call from him.

In early March, Aly, Lorrie, and I flew to Lisbon for the Algarve Cup, joining a national team with a decidedly different look. Mia, Julie, and Joy had retired. Brandi wasn't on the roster. Bri was taking time off. Christie (Pearce) Rampone—now married, though she was always Pearcie to us—was pregnant. Only Kristine Lilly and Kate Markgraf remained from the '99ers, though Abby Wambach was so tight with them you would have thought she had stripped off her own jersey along with them in the Rose Bowl in July 1999.

Greg worked to win us over. April never seemed

to have much fun, and she was always super serious in conversation. Greg was trying to be the exact opposite. He wore sandals and played his guitar for us. He told jokes. He was trying hard to cultivate an image as a fun-loving, laid-back dude who would be an awesome guy to have around. During one of our first team dinners in Portugal, Greg cruised into the room with his guitar. "Hey, who's got a request?" he said, strumming.

Awkward. We all just wanted to finish our meal and go Skype with our friends and boyfriends. We didn't really want to sing "He's Got the Whole World in His Hands" with Greg. This wasn't summer camp. Some of my teammates rolled their eyes. Others applauded, seeing a way to suck up to the new coach. I watched, fascinated but horrified.

Still, Portugal was fun that March. We didn't have a lot of expectations—we were starting a new four-year cycle and a new era. I didn't play the first game—our new goalkeeper coach, Bill Irwin, had worked with Nicole Barnhart when she was a youth player and gave her the start, her first ever in international competition. We won 1–0. I got the next game, against Finland on March 11, 2005, my first national team appearance since September 8, 2002, against Scotland in Columbus, Ohio, when I was a senior in college. That seemed like a long time ago.

I knew that, thanks to two years as a professional player, I was a much better goalkeeper now.

Finland was surprisingly tough for us, but I didn't give up a goal, making four saves. Two days later, I started against Denmark, recording another clean sheet and helping our team to the tournament final against Germany. We won that game 1–0. Our defense was solid in front of me, but I made a few memorable saves, and reports termed it a "coming-out" party for me.

It was definitely a coming-out party for Greg as well, though U.S. Soccer officials said they were conducting a search for a full-time head coach. We would learn that Greg was a pawn in a power struggle. The players were in negotiations for a new contract. U.S. Soccer officials wanted to gain more control over the women's team. Greg didn't have the players' backing, but by hiring him, the federation could send a clear message about who was boss.

We had unwittingly helped his cause. The four shutouts in Portugal were viewed as evidence that Ryan was the right man for the job and that the U.S. team hadn't missed a beat despite the changeover.

Three weeks after we won the Algarve Cup, when I was back in Lyon, Ryan was named the permanent head coach. *Oh well,* I thought with a shrug.

In 2005, the U.S. team continued its transition. One of Greg's first acts as head coach was to tell Brandi

Chastain that her services were no longer needed. Brandi hadn't retired after Athens, and she wanted the chance to try out and see if she could make the team. Greg refused to give it to her, causing an uproar in the press—the heroine of the 1999 World Cup had been fired!—and sending a clear message that this was a new era. I doubted Brandi was still good enough to play, but I felt she deserved the chance to try out. Briana Scurry hadn't officially retired, but the word around the team was that she was thinking about it. I took that with a grain of salt. Bri often needed time off after big tournaments, and I assumed she'd be back. But meanwhile, the starting job was mine.

We had a revolving door of goalkeeper coaches. Greg brought in several different candidates whose main experience had been on youth teams. They were telling us things like, "Make your hands in a W shape to catch the ball." I felt embarrassed: Here we were playing at the highest level, and the coaches were instructing us as if we were in high school. Finally, Ian Feuer, an accomplished goalkeeper and coach, came in. I loved working with Ian, but I knew he wouldn't be around for long: Other teams would happily pay him much more than U.S. Soccer was willing to pay.

Even though the majority of the players in the pool had arrived post-1999, there was still a veteran faction that controlled things. The key movers and shakers of the past were gone, so players like Kate Markgraf and Abby—who acted like a veteran—stepped into the void, taking over decision-making responsibilities for the team. There was definitely a divide on the team between "veterans" and "new players."

I didn't do much to try to win over the veteran group. The longer I was on the national team, the more I realized that my personality and the team dynamic didn't mesh. I didn't want to be best friends with everyone. I didn't want to go to movies or to dinner in huge groups that involved endless planning and negotiations and waiting around. I found it exhausting to be with twenty other women all the time—at training, on the bus, at every meal. I had a difficult time being social twenty-four hours a day. Other girls easily shared their innermost thoughts about boyfriends and family and personal issues, while I liked to keep my private business private. I felt the same as I had in high school: unwilling and unable to play the "social girl" game. But I knew that when I closed my hotel room door so I could watch TV or talk to my dad on the phone and recharge my energy supply, people thought I was being an unfriendly snob.

"People just don't feel like they know you, Hope," Aly once told me.

Around this time, I read a magazine article about introverts. The article was like reading a master's thesis on my personality. Did I prefer spending time alone? Did I enjoy being with just one or two friends? Check. While some people drew energy from others, thriving in big groups, was I exhausted and drained by too much social contact? Check. The article noted that for introverts, trust was a major issue, causing discomfort in groups, and that those trust issues usually dated back to childhood. According to the article, introverts found it hard to feel comfortable and secure in large groups, and while the loudest people were usually viewed as leaders—Abby came quickly to mind—introverts could also lead. I was often called outspoken because I was honest to the point of making others uncomfortable, but I wasn't loud or assertive. I had to figure out how to lead in my own way. Now I had a name for why I felt the way I did, why I preferred to be by myself. I was an introvert. I didn't know that made me a black sheep.

In 2006, Bri returned. She had decided to make one more run, though she would be thirty-six by the time the China World Cup began. I wasn't surprised to see her. Bri had always been nice to me when I was younger and wasn't a threat at all. But now the relationship had changed. There was more tension between us.

"It's your job to lose," Greg told me.

It was strange having a legend behind me, though it wasn't a bad thing: With Briana Scurry in the wings, I couldn't have a bad game. The pressure was on. But it was clear that Bri was going to have to do something extraordinary to win the job. I was far ahead of her in fitness, and the position had evolved in recent years: The kicking game was more important; footwork was emphasized more.

Without a professional league to keep us sharp, U.S. Soccer decided that residency camp was the best way to prepare for the World Cup. In 2006 we started a six-month live-in camp, which meant three weeks at a time training in Southern California and one week at home. During those weeks when I got home, I tried to pack in everything: a trip to Richland to see my family, visits with my dad, local appearances, a coffee with Lesle and Amy. Adrian and I still had our weird connection. I was exhausted.

Our new goalkeeping coach, Mark Dougherty, emphasized fitness, so I excelled with him. At one point, I had a streak of 1,054 minutes without giving up a goal from the run of play, an impressive stretch that ended with a goal by France in the 2006 Algarve Cup. I started every game at the Four Nations Cup in China and was named Goalkeeper of the Tournament. That year, I started eighteen of twenty-two national team games. There wasn't any doubt about who was America's new goalkeeper.

Despite that, I still didn't have the full respect of the veterans. I sensed that the veterans didn't like that Bri had been reduced to the role of backup. Every time Bri made a save, even in practice, they cheered like crazy for her. "Yeah, Bri," Abby would scream when Bri made a routine save. Maybe it was because they'd seen Bri make a comeback before. Or maybe they had a more personal stake in her success—if Bri was being phased out, didn't that make them all expendable?

Everyone in the soccer world had expected a drop-off for our team after most of the stars of '99 departed, yet we still dominated. Under Greg Ryan, we hadn't lost a game. (We lost the 2006 Algarve Cup final on penalty kicks to Germany, but it still counted as a tie.) Though we didn't have the big names, we were still a team that could make America proud.

Residency camp was a revolving door. New players came and went as Greg constantly evaluated new talent.

In spite of his success, Greg began showing signs of insecurity as the year progressed. Instead of the laid-back guy he had tried to be early on, he would get upset about the smallest things: if the balls weren't pumped up right, if the goal was moved.

He was always having conflicts with his staff—the equipment managers and trainers. He didn't seem confident in his own decision-making capabilities.

"Hope," he said to me one day, "let's grab coffee."

As we sat at a local Starbucks, Greg peppered me with questions about our goalkeeping coach. Was I happy with Mark Dougherty? "You're my number one goalkeeper," he said. "I want your opinion."

I liked Mark, but I had some reservations. My fitness was solid, but I believed my technique needed improvement. I felt awkward. "I have incredible respect for Mark," I said. "I think we have a great relationship."

"But?" Greg said. "Come on, Hope, you can be honest. How does he compare to others? We need to do what's best for the team."

I finally conceded that Phil Wheddon was one of the best goalkeeper coaches I had ever worked with. Phil had coached the men's team through the 2006 World Cup in Germany that summer but was now available. I was betraying Mark, but I needed to be honest.

The day after our meeting, Greg fired Mark. I heard later that Greg told Mark that I had come to him saying I wanted Phil back. Rather than taking responsibility as the head coach, he put the decision on me, a twenty-five-year-old goalkeeper. Mark never spoke to me again—and I don't blame him.

New Year's Day, 2007. The Women's World Cup was in September, and I was the team's starting goalkeeper. This was going to be my year. We won the Four Nations Tournament in January in China, which felt like a World Cup preview, and we won the Algarve Cup in March. I was already the second most capped goalkeeper in U.S. history.

On Sunday morning, April 22, hours before the sun rose in California, the draw was held in Wuhan, China. We were placed in the most difficult group of the four, along with Sweden, Nigeria, and North Korea. The inclusion of North Korea infuriated Greg. He had just seen them play China in a predraw match, and their talent was undeniable. The draw appeared to be a political move to keep the North Koreans away from host China. That benefited China but hurt us: We would open against one of the best yet least transparent teams in women's soccer. The only time we had ever played North Korea was in the previous two World Cups. North Korea was hard to scout. Greg was concerned.

But that Sunday morning, the politics of the World Cup draw was the last thing on my mind. My phone rang. "Hope," my mother said, "I have some terrible news about Liz."

My dear friend from high school, Liz Duncan,

had been out for her usual Saturday run near her apartment in Seattle. She stopped on the median of a busy street, waiting for the light to change. A sixteen-year-old in a Pontiac Grand Am lost control of the car, jumped the curb, and ran over Liz. She died at the scene.

I was distraught. Liz and I had been basketball and soccer teammates; we played hard and laughed hard. During college, we were friendly rivals: Liz played soccer for Washington State, and I loved seeing her on the field, trying to score against me. When we were both home from college, she would push me to go on training runs with her, mile after mile in the cold along the Columbia River. She had been a track star at Richland High, and she helped me get in the best shape of my life.

That morning Liz had been doing what she loved best: She ran every single day. I could envision her in a mesh running cap and black running tights, her ponytail swinging behind her. She had just registered for the Chicago Marathon. Her motto was "Life's short. Run long." She was days away from her twenty-seventh birthday.

I called Phil. "I think I need to go home," I said.

I felt tentative, unsure. Could I leave while we were preparing for a World Cup? Was it okay to attend the funeral of one of my best friends? Would my spot be in danger? Would I be letting my team down?

"Hope, if you need to go, go," Phil said.

I did. Some things are more important than soccer.

11

"ONLY A DAUGHTER CRIES LIKE THAT"

ANOTHER HOTEL ROOM. ANOTHER CITY. Another phone ringing.

I rolled out of bed and saw that I had missed a call. I had to stop and think for a moment. What day was it? What city was I in? Why was I here?

Friday, June 15. Cleveland. Tomorrow we had a game against China, the first in our "send-off" series leading to the World Cup. Our pregame meeting was in a few hours. I had been back training with the team for more than a month. After I returned from Liz's funeral, I was reserved, with a singular focus on my training. I wanted to draw inspiration from

115

my strong athletic friend and honor her memory with my effort.

I was going to be late for breakfast. I picked up my phone and saw that I had a message. I had missed a call from a 206 area code. It wasn't a good sign. Who would be calling me at five a.m. Seattle time?

"Hello, Miss Hope Solo?" a businesslike female voice said on the message. "Could you please call us back regarding Jeffrey John Solo?"

Oh God. What had happened? Had someone falsely accused my father again? I had talked to him just a few hours earlier, on Thursday evening.

Full of dread, I called the number. The same abrupt voice answered the phone.

"Hi," I said tentatively. "I'm calling about my dad? Jeffrey John Solo?"

"Oh, yes." She sounded like she was asking for my takeout order. "What kind of arrangement do you want to make for the body?"

My knees buckled, and I sank onto the bed. "What's going on? What are you talking about?"

"I'm sorry," she said. "I thought you'd been informed. Your father passed away, and you're listed as next of kin."

She kept talking, but I couldn't hear her anymore.

"Oh my God, oh my God, oh my God . . ."

My roommate Cat came out of the bathroom and

sat next to me. She figured out what must have happened through my moans. "Hope, you have to get home," she said. "Can you call your family? Do that, and I'll be right back." She went downstairs to tell the team.

I kept telling myself this wasn't real. My dad was supposed to be going on a trip with me in just a few days. On June 23, our team would play Brazil in New York, and Marcus and my father would be there in person to see me play with the national team for the first time.

Oh my God, oh my God.

Shaking, I dialed Marcus's number.

"Wha . . . hello?" Marcus said. I had woken him from a sound sleep.

"Marcus," I said, trying to keep my voice calm. "Dad didn't make it through the night."

My strange wording confused him. It was too hard for me to say that our father had died. When Marcus finally understood what I was trying to tell him, he didn't respond with words but with a guttural, animal-like wail.

I lay curled in a ball while things happened around me in a blur. I couldn't stop crying or shaking. The team manager booked me a flight home. Cat and Aly began to gather my things. My teammates came into the room, one by one, to check on me. Some were unsure how to act and stood awkwardly near the door, simply staring. They had never seen me so vulnerable and broken: I usually presented such a strong front. Marci Miller—older than many of my teammates—seemed to understand what was needed. She sat next to me on the bed and rubbed my leg, murmuring calming words. I latched on to her touch and voice and turned toward her for help. "I don't know what to do," I whimpered. "I can't do this."

I looked up and saw Bri sitting across from me, looking directly into my eyes. "You can do this, Hope," she said. "Be strong."

When I didn't respond, she said again, "You can do this."

Bri had lost her father on Father's Day of 2004, just weeks before the Athens Olympics. She stared intently at me, as though passing her strength and experience through the air between us. I kept my eyes on her. "You can, Hope," Bri said. "You can do this." Then she got up and walked out of the room, like a woman on a mission.

Aly and Cat arranged for a taxi to the airport. As we were leaving my room, Bri returned. She slipped a letter into my hand. "You can do this, Hope," she said again. "You're strong."

At the airport, Aly and Cat checked me in, helped me get into the security line, and hugged me good-bye.

And then I was alone. For years, I had always called my dad before I flew, a ritual to ward off my fear of flying. I couldn't call him now. I was alone with my terrors, old and new.

Memories of my dad rushed at me. Dad holding me up to the basketball hoop in the driveway of the smiley-face house. Dad weeping as he proclaimed his innocence to me in front of REI. Dad reaching out to hug me near a damp Seattle soccer field. Showing me his tent in the woods. Pointing out the sights of Seattle from the top of the Space Needle. Sitting high in the stands in his purple University of Washington sweatshirt. Laughing as he tried to figure out a computer keyboard.

I put my head on my knees and sobbed.

After a few moments, I realized that someone was standing near me. I looked up and saw an unfamiliar man with a kind expression who said, "It's your father, isn't it?"

I nodded, wiping my eyes with my sleeve.

"Only a daughter cries like that for her father."

On the plane I pulled my hood over my head and opened Bri's letter.

She wrote from the heart, describing exactly how I felt. She knew because she had felt the same way— with her heart and soul ripped apart. "It will take time," she wrote, "and, to be honest, it will never go away completely." She encouraged me to hold on to my dad's spirit to help me get through these dark days, to carry him inside me and let myself cry.

"You can do this, yes you can," she wrote. "Do it for both of you."

I remembered that Sunday would be Father's Day.

When I landed at Sea-Tac Airport, Adrian was waiting. He had been the second person I called. He loved my father, and even when things were difficult between us, he had been my dad's favorite. "Don't be upset about Adrian," Dad would tell me. "You two are in love. You just have to work it out."

In recent months, I'd realized my dad was right. I fell into Adrian's arms sobbing, and he wrapped me up.

One blessing was knowing my father's wishes: He had told me and Marcus he wanted to be cremated and have his ashes spread over the Snoqualmie Pass. I hated driving in bad weather, so during the winter, when I had to navigate the pass on my way to Richland, I would stay on the phone with my father until I felt safe. "When I die, scatter my ashes there so I can still look out for you," he had told us.

A few days later, Greg called to find out when I would be back. I told him what I had known all along. I needed to play in the game in New Jersey. It was the moment my father had been looking forward to, and even if he wasn't there, I wanted to fulfill the promise of our trip. I wanted to honor him by playing.

"Greg, I want to play against Brazil," I said. "I'll be there. I'll play."

He hesitated, then launched into minutiae about the travel and practice schedule. He thought I would miss too much training, but I knew the calendar. I knew I would miss only one practice session.

"I'll be there," I said. "I'll play. My dad would want me to."

Despite telling me he would honor my wishes, Greg said, "I think you'll be a distraction to the team. I don't think you'll be emotionally ready. But you can come and sit on the bench with the team." He had made up his mind. He wasn't going to let me play in New Jersey against Brazil.

Everyone helped put together a moving memorial service, including Cheryl, who found photos, helped write the obituary, got the programs printed, and hand-folded them. Many people attended. My father had made a lot of friends, and there was an outpouring of love and respect.

From every person who spoke, we learned something remarkable about my father. When he had been homeless, he had dressed up as Santa every year at the Fred Hutchinson Cancer Research Center, bringing joy to young children who were suffering.

At Hilltop, he'd taught half the residents—men and women—how to play poker, arranging big games for dimes and nickels.

When it was my turn to speak at the memorial, I said that my father often seemed stuck in his ways but that he actually took computer classes to learn how to send me emails when I was away. He spent hours figuring out how to log on to the computer and poking at the keys to come up with a two-line email saying he missed me. Sometimes he would mistakenly erase his finished product and have to start all over. He always laughed at himself when he told me about his technological struggles. In almost every email, he would write the same thing:

Baby Hope, be safe, have fun, go with your vibes, smile and be happy. You are the best. Love, Pops

I told of the secret of his happiness that he had passed along to me. "He guarded each and every memory with his whole heart," I said. "He was fueled by the love he shared with his friends and family, the moments between them, and he relived those happy memories over and over, bringing a new and fresh smile to his face each time. He knew that life could always be worse, so it was important to find joy in the simple things in life. Two things my dad always said to me: 'Baby Hope, go with your vibe. Baby Hope, memories are for you, and nobody can take them away.'"

I ended by saying that my father would always be at my side and in the goal.

After the service, Marcus and I gathered his belongings from his home. We found the objects he had carried from place to place, through the rain and cold, for so many years. A home-run ball Marcus had given him. An etched rock. A signed dollar bill from David from 1977. His carefully maintained scrapbooks were filled with pictures and keepsakes from all four of us: ticket stubs to David's football games, pictures of Terry, a letter from young David telling him about the 1980 Lakers-Sonics playoff games that ended with a plaintive, "I miss you, Dad, I really love you a lot, Dad." There were clippings about Dominic Woody's minor league baseball career—my dad had coached him back in Richland. There were letters in childish blocky writing to him from Marcus and me. My dad kept everything, carrying it with him for years through the Seattle rain. He had catalogued it all and written little notes with observations and messages of love for his children.

Another scrapbook was filled with newspaper clippings, photos, and computer printouts detailing my entire soccer career, from Richland High to UW to the WUSA and all my time with the national team. Everything was arranged in chronological order and carefully annotated. There was a Christmas card from Sofia, to "Mr. Italy," as she called my dad. I turned it to the last page of the scrapbook. At the top, in my father's blocky handwriting, he had written HOPE: WORLD CUP, 2007.

The page was blank.

12

SHADOWS

GREG REFUSED TO BUDGE ABOUT my playing against Brazil. My teammates—even Bri, who would get the start instead of me—thought he was being unreasonable. I knew that, given the chance, I would play with strength and inspiration; I thought of how NFL quarterback Brett Favre had played just a day after his own father had died. I had faith that I could play well through my emotions and sadness. I always had before.

But Greg insisted that I was mentally unprepared, so I decided I would play the part he had assigned me. I would grieve, and sit in the stands with my mom and Marcus, who had made the trip to support me. On June 23, I watched my team play Brazil. My teammates wore black armbands for my dad. Bri kept his initials on her goalie gloves. We quickly went up 2–0. Both goals were scored on free kicks, one by Kristine Lilly and another that Cat took and Abby headed in. Our team rolled to victory.

During training back in California, Greg was pushing me hard every day. We would leave for China in less than eight weeks. My grief was near the surface. On the bus I sat by myself, staring out the window and listening to music. Tears trickled down my cheeks. I didn't talk much to anyone; I felt as though every time I opened my mouth I might cry.

But the tears dried up on the field. My eyes were clear while I zeroed in on shots. I was so focused that the pain went away. Soccer training was once again what it had been when I was young: a chance to block out everything bad in my life for the few hours I was on the field.

One day we had a team-building exercise: We all taped sheets of paper to our backs and then went from teammate to teammate writing what we liked about that person. The comments were anonymous. At the end of the exercise, we took off the paper. Mine was filled with positive messages.

"You are such a force. We believe in you so
     much."
"Your communication on and off the field, all
     the great advice you've given me, plus how
     strong you are."
"Always striving for more and pushing this
     team to be its best."
"Hopers—you are always the one I can talk to.
     You are one of my best friends."
"You are strong and courageous and you have
     made me a better person."
"You have pushed me to be better. Just know
     your dad is always watching."

I was back in goal for our next game against
Norway, on July 14 in Connecticut. Marcus and I had
each taken a small container of our father's ashes
and kept them with us all the time. Marcus took my
dad fishing. I carried my dad with me into the locker
room. After all, he had always joked that he was
helping me out in goal while he watched my games
on television. "I'm going to trip those forwards for
you," he would say gleefully.

I needed him to be right beside me, tripping
forwards. We shut out Norway, 1–0.

I missed talking to him. He was the one who
could comfort me, who could put all the pressure

in perspective and make me laugh. He understood sports and knew what to say. Unable to call him as the biggest tournament of my life approached, I started writing to him in a journal.

July 15, 2007

Here I am sitting aboard a flight coming back home to Seattle. Seattle doesn't feel like home without you there. No longer do I have a place to go to just talk, laugh, cry, eat, or nap. This year, Dad—my first World Cup—I dedicate to you. You're coming to China with me and you're going to help me tend that goal. It was good to get back on the field after taking three weeks off. We shut out Norway together, didn't we? I've never felt so at ease in the net. I didn't have a care in the world. I want to make your legacy live on.

You are so right that any time I feel lonely I can pull a memory out and then lock it back up for the next time I need it. Nobody can take my memories away. You've taught me so well, Dad. You have prepared me for life. You have taught me how to fight, how to love deeply, how not to get bullied, how to reach out to others, how not to judge, how to enjoy life, how to be happy no matter where I walk. You have

taught me to be me, and you are such a part of
me. I will carry your spirit inside me no matter
whcre I go.

  I love you, Dad.

I had worked all my life for this moment, to make my father and the rest of my family proud, to fulfill my destiny. I was ready. I was in the best shape of my life, and I was proving it every day in practice. I felt confident in directing the defense, barking out orders.

Our last game in the States was a 4–0 victory over Finland. We still hadn't lost a game in regulation since Greg had taken over as coach. We'd played forty-six games under Greg, and I had started thirty-six of them. We were issued gold World Cup uniforms. The message was clear: Nothing less than a gold medal was acceptable.

Despite our record and gold shorts, we were leaving for China with little fanfare. Nike's ad campaign for the World Cup was "The Greatest Team You've Never Heard Of," which was an accurate description. While the American public could still name Mia Hamm and Brandi Chastain, we were strangers. We were still in the shadow of the '99ers. We were determined to change that—we were going to make our own history. On August 27, we boarded a plane in Los Angeles headed for Shanghai. My heart was heavy, but my resolve had never been stronger.

This was my moment. Nothing was going to get in the way.

13

"YOU CAN'T GO BY A GUT FEELING"

IT WAS THE MORNING OF my first World Cup game.

The ashes were in a small container the size of my thumb that I placed in my locker before every game. Though I normally wouldn't wear my goalkeeper gloves out to the field, I did in China, continuing the ritual I had started in my first game back after my father died. I placed a tiny bit of ash in my left glove in the locker room. Out on the field, I put my right hand over my heart for the national anthem and held my left glove carefully by my side. When I walked into the goal, I made the sign of the cross, kissed my closed fist, then opened my glove and let the ashes drop, saying a little prayer to myself. I had meant what I had said at his memorial: My dad would always be in goal with me.

That morning I had written in my journal.

> *Dad,*
> *Game day, not sure how I feel. A little queasy but been that way for days. I feel my heart beating against the mattress. I miss you, Dad. Help me live the moment. Dad, I love you so much. Wearing your armband. Got you with me. Picture in locker, bracelet and necklace on, ashes in goal, me and my dad in goal together.*

We played a scoreless first half; I had a breakaway save and came out to stop some through balls, cutting off their relentless attack. Soon after halftime, Abby put us on the board, hammering a pass from Kristine Lilly that skipped off the North Korean goalkeeper's gloves and into the net. It was glaring evidence of what I already knew: the conditions were rough for goalkeepers. The field was soaked, the ball was heavy, and the slippery new commemorative design on the ball's surface only made it harder to handle.

Minutes after giving us the lead, Abby collided with a North Korean player and fell to the ground, blood gushing from a gash in her head. She went off for stitches as play continued, but Greg didn't replace her. We kept glancing to the sideline to see if a sub was coming on but continued to play a woman down. North Korea—already far too comfortable—was clearly energized by Greg's decision to let us play shorthanded until Abby could return and stepped up the pressure. The North Koreans passed the ball with ease in front of our goal, eventually sending a pass wide to Kil Son Hui at the top of the penalty box. She arced the ball toward me.

"You're fine! You're fine!"

I could hear Kate Markgraf screaming at me. The wet ball had just slipped off my fingertips and over my head, into the net.

A goal. In the very first game of the World Cup. I threw up my hands and shouted in frustration. We were tied 1–1 with North Korea in the second period on a wet, slippery field in Chengdu.

"Okay, okay," I told myself. "Come on, Hope." I was more angry than rattled. Our opening game wasn't going well.

Abby had been out for three minutes, and we were tied and struggling. Yet Greg still continued to let us play shorthanded. The message he was sending was pretty clear: *Without Abby, we're doomed. Our subs are no good.*

I gathered my composure but was still under

incredible pressure. The North Korean players played kickball with one another while our team struggled for possession. After Carli Lloyd was called for a foul, North Korea sent a free kick wide of the goal and then passed the ball among six different players. A shot heading toward the right post was deflected by Shannon Boxx directly in front of me; I was moving right, then tracked left with the deflection. But Kim Yong-Ae pounced on the ball and shot it over my outstretched right hand.

Another goal. There was nothing I could have done on that one. We were down 2–1. We had never lost a game in group play in World Cup history. I could see the alarm in my teammates' eyes. Greg seemed paralyzed on the sideline, doing nothing to stop North Korea's momentum. Finally, after ten long minutes and two North Korean goals, Abby came sprinting out onto the field with eleven stitches in her head. Back at full strength, we calmed down. In the sixty-ninth minute, Heather O'Reilly buried a shot in the upper right corner of the net. We were even, 2–2, but North Korea continued to push forward. In stoppage time, they thought they had the winner on a hard shot, but I fully extended to my right to push the ball out of danger. Just seconds later, another North Korean player took a long shot directly on goal that I dove at and smothered. Finally the whistle blew. We finished with a draw and a critical point in the group standings.

I wasn't happy about the goals—particularly the first one that had slipped off my gloves—but I was still proud. I had made a fistful of spectacular saves that kept our team in the game. I learned a rough lesson about trying to catch a slippery ball, a mistake I wouldn't make again. We came away with a point on a day when no one—not me, our field players, our coach—was at their best. Coming up big in the final seconds of the game only bolstered my confidence.

After the whistle, Greg came up to me on the field. He had a huge grin on his face. "Thank you for those saves," he said, giving me a hug. Then he pointed to the sky. "Somebody's watching out over you from up there," he said.

After the North Korea game, we stayed in gray Chengdu—a city famous for its lack of sunshine—for another few days to play Sweden, the third-ranked team in the world.

Sept 14, 2007

Game Two—so nervous, Dad. Please be with me. Help me know that I have nothing to prove after last game. Help me to live in the moment. Right through the fingers, Dad, but I played so well. I just want to play relaxed, play in the moment, enjoy every minute. Let's have fun, Dad.

Our game against Sweden was a much better outing for our team, with none of the tension and dramatics of the North Korea game. Abby scored twice, the first goal coming on a penalty kick, and our defense played much better. I saw my old friend Lotta Schelin—the rising star of the Swedish team—but she couldn't beat me. I had my first World Cup victory and shutout. I whispered a word of thanks to my dad.

We left Chengdu and headed to Shanghai, getting into the city just days before Typhoon Wipha. We played Nigeria—with the chance to win our group—in a steady downpour. Lori Chalupny scored just fifty-three seconds into the match, and Nigeria was on its heels the rest of the day. Still, late in the game, I was forced to make some saves to preserve the victory. Another shutout.

Despite our difficult draw, we had won our group and were now in the quarterfinals against England. The game was in Tianjin, in northern China, a long trek from Shanghai. All our family members made the journey. The night before the game, I went over to the family hotel. My big support group had arrived in time for the Nigeria game: my mother, Marcus and his fiancée Debbie, Aunt Susie, Grandma Alice and

Grandpa Pete, Adrian, and Cheryl's parents, Mary and Dick. At the games, they wore black armbands to honor my father. It was comforting for me to be with my family. They were the only ones who really knew how much I missed my father and how badly I was hurting. I was painfully aware of all the time I had missed with him, rushing from one place to another, moments I could never get back. I wasn't going to make that same mistake with the rest of my family. And we all had something to celebrate in China: Marcus and Debbie had just found out they were going to have a baby.

Sept. 22, 2007

Hey, Dad. Why is today so hard? I'm scared today. Marcus is scared. I'm glad we could be together even just for a little bit—he's very emotional. Wants us to go all the way for you. Be there beside me in that lonesome goal. We play together in this quarterfinal match against England. But I play for you, for everything that you taught me. Family first, right, Dad?

England's team hadn't had much success at the senior level—this was the first time we had faced them in a World Cup match—but they were touted as an up-and-coming team. I considered Kelly Smith, whom I'd played with in Philadelphia, one of the top players in the world. We had a tense, scoreless first half—but our defense was strong. And then, in a ten-minute span in the second half, we scored three quick goals to put the game out of reach.

After the game, our celebration was subdued, tempered by our ambitions. We were almost to our ultimate goal. We were in the World Cup semifinals, as far as the 2003 team had advanced, but we wanted more.

We would face Brazil, a team that had appeared disorganized and unprepared in New Jersey just three months earlier. I had three consecutive World Cup shutouts. I was on top of my game. I was ready.

On Tuesday night, two days before the semifinal, we were eating dinner at the team hotel in Hangzhou. One of my first starts had come in Hangzhou in January 2001. That seemed so long ago.

Phil came up behind me as I was eating and tapped me on the shoulder. "Hope," he said, bending down to speak in my ear. "Greg wants to see you in his room when dinner is over."

I stared at him. The balloon of confidence inside me collapsed. "Why?" I asked.

Phil just looked at me and then walked away.

I pushed away my food, suddenly afraid I might get sick.

I took the elevator to Greg's floor. When I entered his room, he was sitting in a chair, playing his guitar and singing to himself. "Hey, Hope, do you know this song?" He smiled and strummed.

Seriously? He wanted to chat about Pink Floyd? I just looked at him. *Don't mess with me, Greg,* I thought. I'm sure my face gave away my thoughts. When he saw my expression, Greg became a tough guy.

"Why are you late? I told you to be here at seven."

I looked at Phil, who was sitting at the other end of the couch. "Actually, I was told to come after dinner," I said.

I put my hands on my knees and looked down at them, taking a deep breath to steady myself. Greg leaned forward and stuck his finger in my face. "You look at me when I'm talking to you," he snapped. "I'm tired of you disrespecting me. You show up late and now you don't even make eye contact with me."

I was shocked. I knew this was going to be bad, but the fury in his voice stunned me. *Okay,* I thought, *you want me to look at you?* I looked down again, gathered myself, and slowly turned my head to stare at him, never breaking eye contact as he derailed my career.

I wasn't ready for a major tournament, Greg said. He'd suspected it all along. And he could tell that in the first game when the ball went off my hands. He should have benched me after that soft goal. Bri had a winning record against Brazil, Greg said. She matched up better with Brazil's style. She single-handedly won the gold medal in the 2004 Olympics against Brazil. And she had just played Brazil in New Jersey.

I watched his mouth move. I heard the words coming out of it. I could see how they'd be printed in the newspapers, replayed on ESPN, crafted into headlines and sound bites. *Briana Scurry, one of the heroes of the 1999 World Cup, wins back her spot in goal.*

I was numb. Greg was waiting for a response. I didn't want to give him the satisfaction of weeping or raging. I worked hard to channel my fury into clear, precise words. "Greg, I have to respect your decision because you're my coach," I said. "But I disagree with you. It doesn't matter what Bri did three years ago. She hasn't played a game for more than three months, she hasn't been your number one for three years, and I'm playing the best I've ever played. I will never agree with your decision. And if anyone asks me, I will tell them that this is the wrong decision."

Greg smiled. He was back to being the cool guy. "That's why I love you, Hope," he said. "I expect my athletes to want to be on the field. To be angry if they don't play. I've given you four World Cup games. I've gotten you this far."

"*I've* gotten myself this far," I snapped. "Plenty of

people—well before you came along—have believed in me along the way."

He wasn't finished. "You know, Hope, this wasn't just my decision," he said. "Lil and Abby came to me. They want Bri to play. I agree with the captains. It's a gut feeling."

There had been a meeting behind my back? A decision based on whom they liked better? I shook my head in disgust. He was a weak leader. He was ditching responsibility. Greg didn't have the nerve to stand up for his decisions. He was passing the buck to the players.

"You can't go by a gut feeling, Greg," I said. "I've been your starting goalkeeper for three years. And now, in the biggest game of the tournament, you're pulling me because your gut tells you to?"

Greg didn't like my tone. I wasn't crying. I wasn't folding. I wasn't making it easy. Instead, I was fighting back with words and logic, keeping my emotions tacked down. So he tried to provoke me. "You haven't been training well," he said. "You got killed today in practice. I brought the other coaches to watch. You had three times the amount of goals scored on you as Bri did."

He could make up whatever reasons he wanted, but he couldn't attack my work ethic. He had told all the starters to take it easy in practice after the England game. We'd had four draining games in eleven days in the muggy monsoons of China. We had been told to rest our bodies. I was nursing a triceps strain and—for the first time in my career—I was trying to heed the advice of our trainers and be professional about being careful with an injury. I wasn't the only one holding back. Bri, on the other hand, hadn't played in three months—of course she was going all out.

I looked over at Phil. I didn't know what to say. Logic was out the window. Greg was all over the place, his reasons for benching me shifting every time he opened his mouth. There was clearly no use arguing. He was panicking. And I was paying the price.

We were both silent. I had nothing left to say, so I stood up to leave. Greg leaned over and pushed me back down on the couch. Hard. "You leave when I say you can leave," he said.

I was stunned that he had gotten physical with me. I wanted to lash back, to hit him hard. For a split second I really thought I would—I felt my hand move forward. But I wasn't going to let him provoke me. I restrained myself and glanced over at Phil, glad to have a witness. "Are we done?" I said icily. "Can I leave now?"

I walked out of the room and down the hallway to find Kristine Lilly. Lil was playing in her fifth

World Cup. She was the last of the veterans from the first World Cup in 1991. We had never been close, but I respected her ability. I wasn't intimidated. She needed to hear me out.

"Lil, I've been your starting goalkeeper for three years. How can you decide—in the semifinals of the World Cup—that you want another goalkeeper?"

Lil looked shocked, as though she'd never expected Greg to reveal their private conversation. She certainly didn't seem prepared for a confrontation. "I—I don't think it matters who's in goal," she stammered.

"Lil, you're our captain," I said. "It should matter to you who's in goal. You should have an opinion. But if you don't think it even matters at all, how can you go and lobby for Bri?"

I thought I saw a flutter of doubt cross her eyes. Had she made a mistake? "I'm your starting goalkeeper for a reason," I went on. "Because I beat out the others. You should want the best players on the field. It's so arrogant to say that it doesn't matter who's in goal." I wasn't yelling. I was calm. "I've lost every ounce of respect I had for you," I said.

I walked away. I went farther down the hall to find Abby and told her exactly what I had told Lil. I felt even more betrayed by Abby—she and I were in the same generation of players.

"How could you turn your back on me?" I said.

At least Abby had an answer. "Hope, I think Bri is the better goalkeeper."

That shut me up. I didn't think it was true, and I didn't think Abby knew much about goalkeeping. But at least she had an opinion. At least she owned up to her part in the matter. I had to respect that.

I went back to my room and called my mother. "I'm not playing against Brazil, Mom," I said, crying.

"Liar," my mother said with a laugh.

I wasn't lying. I wasn't having a bad dream. I lay on my bed and wept.

> *Sept. 27, 2007*
>
> *Best in the world, Dad? I'm not so sure the world will see that. Can you believe this is the semifinal game and I'll be on the bench? I need you there with me too, Dad. What's going to happen, Dad? Has my career ended with the game against England? Dad, it's tough. My fight has been crushed. Please help me and Marcus get through this, Dad. I still play for you. With all my love—Baby Hope*

On Thursday, September 27, the news that I had lost my starting job was being talked about back home, on blogs and sports shows. ESPN's commentators—Julie Foudy and former U.S. coach

Tony DiCicco—expressed amazement at Greg's decision. Why would someone make such a radical change when things were going so well? "It makes a negative impact when you want to only be focusing on positive things," Julie said. "I think it's the wrong decision."

DiCicco agreed. "If there isn't a goalkeeper controversy, why make one?"

"This is the type of decision that keeps you employed or quickly gets you unemployed," ESPN commentator Rob Stone offered.

Because of the time difference, our games were airing at dawn in the United States. Back in Seattle, where it was still dark, Lesle Gallimore turned on the television. "Hope Solo replaced in goal by Briana Scurry." She fumbled for her phone to call Amy. "Is Hope hurt? What's going on?"

I refused to have my dad beside me on the bench. I didn't carry ashes with me onto the field in Hangzhou.

The game was a disaster almost from the start. Bri looked rusty, colliding with Brazilian forward Formiga as she came out on a free kick. In the twentieth minute, U.S. defender Leslie Osborne dove to head away a corner kick and ended up knocking the ball past Bri and into the net.

An own goal, the most demoralizing play in soccer. We were trailing 1–0.

Seven minutes later, Marta—the most feared player in the world—dribbled down the right flank and was fouled by one of our defenders, who grabbed her shorts. Marta wriggled out of the grasp and blasted a shot into the lower right corner of the net. Bri dove and got a hand on it but couldn't keep the ball from slipping past her. On the television broadcast, DiCicco told viewers that it was exactly the kind of shot Bri had once always stopped. "If she's on her game, she makes this save," he said.

We were down 2–0, and it was about to get worse. In stoppage time of the first half, Shannon Boxx received her second yellow card of the game for taking down Brazilian forward Cristiane. It was a questionable call, but there was no appealing the referee's decision. Boxx was sent off, and our team was going to have to play the entire second half a player short—ten versus eleven—for forty-five minutes.

I was distraught. I couldn't believe how poorly our team was playing—at every position. I knew we were so much better than this.

Watching from the bench in the second half, I witnessed the complete collapse of my team and our four-year dream. Eleven minutes into the second half, our defense was out of position and Cristiane flicked in another goal. Brazil 3, USA 0.

I sat at the end of the bench, stunned and angry.

At one point, my teammate Natasha Kai leaned over and nudged me. "Hey," she said. "The cameras are on you."

"I don't care," I told her. Was I supposed to act fine as our dream derailed?

The last blow came in the seventy-ninth minute with one of the most beautiful goals in World Cup history, a dazzling play by Marta, who sent the ball over her shoulder, caught up with it, and spun past our defense to make it 4–0.

An eternity later, the whistle finally blew. The Brazilian players celebrated wildly at midfield. I had just one mission—to make my way over to where my family was sitting in the stands. As I crossed the field, Abby Wambach approached me. She looked me straight in the eye. "Hope," she said, "I was wrong."

I looked down and nodded. What could I say? The evidence was lit up on the scoreboard. Abby gave me a quick, hard embrace, and we walked away in separate directions.

I crossed the field to my family. Marcus leaned over the railing toward me, the pain showing on his face. In his hands he held tight his container of my father's ashes. "This was supposed to be for Dad," he said.

That broke me open. I wanted so much to be strong for my family, to honor our father. I ached to make them proud. And now there was only more hurt. But I drew strength just being near my family. I reached up to squeeze their hands and say good-bye. A security guard came to get me—I was the last player on the field.

14

STEPPING INTO LIQUID

AT INTERNATIONAL SOCCER GAMES, PLAYERS exit the stadium through the "mixed zone," an area where reporters gather for postgame interviews. They line up on one side of metal barricades, and the players walk through on the other side. Our press officer, Aaron Heifetz, stuck next to me. When someone reached out to me across the barrier, Heifetz announced in a loud voice, "She didn't play. You only want to talk to people who played the game."

One thing I've learned in my life is that I can speak for myself, that I can fight my own battles. I don't like anyone telling me how I'm supposed to feel or think or what I'm supposed to say. If I had meekly accepted what others told me, my life would be radically different: I would have gone to a different school. I never would have reconnected with my father. I would be estranged from my mother. I would have viewed myself as a failure.

I turned to Aaron. "Heif, this is *my* decision."

I stepped toward the microphone and, in an instant, broke an unwritten code that declares female athletes don't make waves. We don't criticize. Our hard competitive edges are always smoothed down for public display.

"It was the wrong decision," I said, my voice shaking with emotion. "And I think anybody who knows anything about the game knows that."

I was speaking into a microphone, but I was talking directly to Greg Ryan. "There's no doubt in my mind I would have made those saves," I said. "And the fact of the matter is, it's not 2004 anymore. It's 2007, and I think you have to live in the present. And you can't live by big names. You can't live in the past. It doesn't matter what somebody did in an Olympic gold medal game three years ago. *Now* is what matters, and that's what I think."

I turned and walked away, an angry Heifetz on my heels. He lectured me harshly for speaking out as we boarded the team bus. I told him that if he didn't want me to answer questions, he shouldn't have taken me past reporters.

I went to my usual spot in the back, where I always sat with my closest friends on the team. The mood was grim; everyone was in shock. We hadn't lost a game in more than three years. The conversation was muted.

"You guys," I told them, "I just did an interview."

"What did you say?"

"I said I believed I would have made those saves."

"Uh-oh, Hope," someone said with a laugh.

"I'm sure it's fine," Carli said.

"I don't know if it is," I said, and put my earbuds in.

It didn't feel like anything was fine. Our team had just suffered its worst World Cup loss in history, our first loss in almost three years. In ninety minutes, everything we had worked for had been erased.

The bus pulled out of the stadium and took us to our Hangzhou hotel. The plan was to eat and have a quick visit with our families before the long bus ride back to Shanghai. While we were in the lobby, the Brazilian team and their supporters came in. They were at the same hotel, a boneheaded move on the part of the Chinese organizers. The Brazilians danced around the lobby, doing the samba, beating their drums, snaking through the small groups of

American supporters. You could feel the tension rise—I wouldn't have been surprised if a fight broke out. Brazil was celebrating in that uniquely Brazilian way, but they were rubbing our noses in the loss.

Soon we got back on the bus to ride through the night to Shanghai, where we would play a third-place game in a few days.

Carli texted with her trainer, James, in New Jersey. She turned to me. "Hope, James says this is blowing up back home," she said. "It's all over the news."

"What is?"

"Your interview."

I stared out the window, watching the lights rush past in the dark night, replaying my words in my head. I had said what I thought about Greg's decision—I assumed he had told the press his reasoning for starting Bri. I knew it was rare for a player to criticize a coach, but I felt justified in stating my point of view.

Once we got to the Westin Shanghai, Carli and Marci Miller—whom I roomed with in Shanghai— huddled with me in front of the computer. We found the interview on ESPN and watched it. "It's not so bad, is it?" I asked them. "That was meant for Greg, not Bri."

Carli and Marci hesitantly agreed. No, it wasn't horrible.

"Well," I said, trying to laugh, "I guess it's only a

matter of time before I get hell from the older players."

Right then, my phone rang. "I guarantee you this is them," I said as I picked up.

It was Lil. "Hope, we want to talk to you. Can you come to our room?"

I walked down the hall. By now it was after midnight. I pushed open the door of Lil's room and saw the veterans grimly waiting for me. Kate Markgraf stood by the door. Lil, Shannon Boxx, Christie Rampone, Abby, and Bri sat on the beds. I walked across to other side of the room and leaned against the wall.

"We saw your interview," Lil said. "We don't think that's what you do on this team."

"Well, I'm a professional athlete—of course I believe I could make a difference on the field," I said. "Just like you guys do," I added. "We should all believe we can make a difference, or else why are we professional athletes?"

Kate Markgraf turned on me. "I can't even look at you," she said. "Who do you think you are? I can't even be in the same room with you."

She walked out and slammed the door. *Wow,* I thought, *that seems overly dramatic.*

Now there were five. They told me that you don't throw a teammate under the bus, that I had broken the code, that I had betrayed the team. "You've ruined everything this team was built on," Abby said. "What Julie Foudy and Mia and Lil and all the players who paved the way for us made—you've torn it all down." Abby had already said she had been wrong. She knew Greg had messed up everything.

"Abby, this isn't about Julie Foudy or anyone else from the past," I said. "This is about our team. I would never do anything to hurt Bri. I have so much respect for her. But as a professional athlete, I'm confident that I would have made a difference in the game. I believe in myself enough to know that I would have made a difference. I think all of us believe in ourselves enough to think we can make a difference."

"Are you even going to apologize to Bri?" Abby said.

I turned toward Bri. I wanted her to know that I wasn't trying to hurt her, not after everything she had done for me when my father died. I felt backed against the wall.

Bri spoke first. She told me I had hurt her very much. She said she had tried to be there for me when my father died and was shocked that I would do this to her.

"I'm sorry, Bri," I said. "I really am. I didn't mean to hurt you. My comments were directed at Greg, not at you."

I could tell how awkward I sounded. I wanted to

have a private moment with Bri, but I was in a room full of angry women who demanded that I perform a public act of remorse. Everything felt forced. Staged.

"Hope, we've heard your side of things," Christie Rampone said. "You've heard how we feel. So how are we going to move forward and make this better?"

I looked at her with gratitude. Pearcie was the only one trying to lead us through the mess, to cut through the harsh words and angry feelings. The group decided that the way to move forward was for me to apologize to the entire team. There would be a team meeting in the morning.

I went back to my room for a few tortured hours. I couldn't sleep. I cried most of the night and tried to figure out what to do. All my life I've said exactly what I thought and stood up for myself. But now I was in a firestorm for doing just that. I felt terrible that I had hurt Bri. She had been so kind to me when my father died. I vowed to talk to her in the morning and try to make things right between us.

The next morning, Cat came to my room before the meeting. "Hope, just apologize from your heart," she said.

When I stepped into the room and saw Bri standing by the door, I paused. "Bri, do you have a second?" I said. "Please know I would never want to hurt you. I have so much respect for you."

She turned away from me. "Hope, I can't even look at you right now," she said.

Okay, I thought. *This is going to take time. This is going to be on Bri's terms. I have to just keep trying.*

I walked into the room and felt twenty sets of eyes bore into me. I was onstage. I said the same thing I had said to the smaller group in Lil's room the night before. "I never meant to hurt Bri," I said. "My comments were directed at Greg and his reasoning. I said I would have made those saves because I truly have to believe I could have made a difference."

I didn't see any sign of support. I saw hostility and anger. Hatred, even. Hard words were flung at me.

"You don't sound sincere."

"Do you even care what you've done?"

"How can you turn your back on the team?"

"Do you know how horrible you looked on television, pouting on the bench?"

"You've been feeling sorry for yourself since Greg told you that you weren't starting. All you could do was cry. Some of us sit on the bench every game."

I looked at my few close friends, hoping for a sympathetic face. Aly and Cat just stared at me. I looked at the faces of the younger players, like Leslie Osborne and Lori Chalupny and Tina Frimpong, my former UW teammate. I had become an outcast. Everyone was following Lil and Abby. No one would stand up for me. Only Carli seemed to have any sympathy in her expression.

"You haven't even apologized to Bri," someone said.

I had already apologized to Bri in Lil's room the night before. I had just spoken to her again outside the door. But I apologized to Bri again, in front of everyone. I had maintained my composure through most of the meeting, but as I spoke, I started to cry. "I'm sorry, Bri," I said. "I never meant to hurt you. I'm sorry that I did."

I was asked to leave the room while my fate was decided.

Later that day, Greg called me into his room. He was smiling and friendly as he told me I was suspended. "Hope, I did a lot of bad things in my playing career," he said, then told me a story about how he'd stormed off the field after getting subbed out in a game. "You get through them; you move on. That said, I don't know how this is going to go for you, because you let your teammates down with your comments."

On Saturday, the day before the third-place game, I was left behind at the hotel while the team went to training. Our massage therapist, Kara Mirarchi, stayed to babysit me. I'm not sure what they were afraid would happen if I were left alone: That I would call the press? Rifle through my teammates' belongings? Harm myself?

I really wanted to be alone, but Kara thought it would be calming to watch a surf movie. She tried to make me comfortable. We watched *Step into Liquid*. I felt like I was in prison.

Our general manager, Cheryl Bailey, met with me after training. She had more bad news. "You can't fly home with the team on Monday."

All I wanted was to get home as quickly as possible. Instead, I would have to wait for more than half a day after everyone else left China before I could get a flight home late Monday night.

That afternoon, there was a press conference. "We did not have Hope attend practice today," Greg said. "She will not be attending the game tomorrow. We have moved forward with twenty players who have stood by each other, who have battled for each other, and when the hard times came—and the Brazil game was a hard time—they stood strong."

Lil spoke. "How we look at everything with our group is we do what's best for the team," she said. "And what is best for the team is the twenty of us right now. I think the circumstance that happened and her going public has affected the whole group. I think having her with us is still a distraction."

Yes, I was definitely a distraction—a *welcome* distraction from having to face up to the disaster of the Brazil game. As long as the focus was on me, Greg wasn't held accountable. The horrible loss wasn't the headline.

On the day of the final World Cup games, I went for breakfast at the family hotel. In the lobby, I ran into Sunil Gulati, president of U.S. Soccer. "Hope, come up to my room and chat for a minute," he said.

My heart sank. Sunil was the head of the federation. Was I going to be kicked off the team? Was I in for another lecture?

No, Sunil was friendly. He introduced me to his wife, Marcela. He didn't scold me. "I just want to see how you're doing," he said.

"You know," Sunil added, "if this had happened on a men's team, I think it would be quite a different situation." He pretended to throw a punch, implying that's how men would deal with it. "If you need anything, let me know," he said with a friendly smile.

The head of U.S. Soccer wasn't excluding me. That was one small bit of good news.

During the matches, I was confined to my hotel. My mother and Adrian stayed with me. "If my daughter's not allowed to be there, I won't be there either," my mom said. But the rest of my supporters went. My grandma wore her big billboard pin, which she could program to flash different names. It usually flashed HOPE NO. 18, but now she made it read BRI NO.1. My family wanted to show their support for Bri, to make it clear that what I'd said wasn't directed at Bri.

Back at the hotel, Adrian and Mom and I watched the games on a tiny television. My teammates easily beat Norway and then celebrated as though they had won the World Cup. Abby scored two goals and ran to the bench for team high fives, which looked to me like a staged moment to prove that all twenty were a team. When Lilly came out in the eighty-ninth minute, there was a big show of giving Bri the captain's armband. It seemed like an act for the cameras.

In the final, Germany shut down Marta and easily handled Brazil.

The next morning, my team packed up and left China while I sat in my room. My family left while I stayed alone in the hotel for hours, waiting for my late-night flight. When I left for the airport, it was the first time I had been out of either the team or family hotel since arriving in Shanghai, almost ninety-six hours earlier.

When I got in line to check in, I saw that I was on a flight with many U.S. team supporters and friends and boyfriends. I wanted to hide from them. But I couldn't. "I can't believe what happened to you," one man said. "I don't know how Ryan could bench one of the best goalkeepers in the world."

I was surprised. "Thank you," I said.

"Hang in there, Hope," another stranger said. "It's such a shame."

"We're rooting for you," his wife said.

I boarded the plane, sank into my seat, and left China behind.

15

"DON'T LET THE DEVIL STEAL YOUR JOY"

BACK HOME, ISOLATED IN A little cabin I'd bought in Kirkland, I barely ate. I ignored my ringing phone. I didn't want to turn on my computer. The one person I wanted to talk to was gone. My father was dead, and his absence—now without the distraction of the World Cup—overwhelmed me. I was paralyzed.

I thought about my grandmother and her capacity for forgiveness. She said anger and hate were poison to the soul: "Don't let the devil steal your joy."

My phone kept ringing. All day, every day. Finally I answered it. It was my agent, Rich. He wanted me to join a conference call with the U.S. Soccer bosses,

Sunil Gulati and Dan Flynn. And Greg Ryan.

The team had a "celebration tour" beginning on October 13 in St. Louis—just days away. It was supposed to be a victory tour, but we hadn't won anything. Still, there were three games scheduled against Mexico in three different cities. "Rich, I don't want to get on the call. I don't want to go on this tour," I said. "I don't have the strength or energy. I don't want to go through all of this again."

Rich calmly said that was fine. He said he'd support me no matter what I decided. But he also told me I should get on the call and tell Sunil and Dan. This was about my career.

I was beginning to understand that what happened at the World Cup had been huge news on sports networks and talk radio, unheard of for women's soccer, especially during football season. I was learning that many thought Greg's transgression and the team's behavior were far worse than my outburst. The shunning of Hope Solo was discussed nationwide, on TV sports shows and late-night comedy shows. Damage control was needed.

The Monday before the tour, I sat on my couch with the phone against my ear. I listened to Sunil and Dan speak about the victory tour, about the need to be professional. Then it was Greg's turn. He talked about how important it was for me to show real regret. He pointed out that Marion Jones had given back her Olympic medals out of shame for doping. He suggested that I give back my tour money or my bronze medal if I wanted to show true remorse. He said that I wouldn't be on the national team without him, that he had given me my opportunity.

"Greg, I've been in this program since 1999," I said. "I've been the starting goalkeeper on every age-level team for this country. You are not the one who opened doors for me. I've been with the national team longer than you've been here, and I'll remain in it longer than you do. I don't owe my starting spot to you: I earned it."

I decided then that I wanted to be on the tour. "I'm going to be a part of the celebration," I added. "Contractually it's my right to be there."

"The team doesn't want you there," Greg said.

"Well, it's not up to the team anymore," I said. "I'm going to be there. I'm going to put myself through hell by being there, but I need to start this process."

I looked at a framed picture on my table of Grandma Alice and Grandpa Pete hugging me. "'Refuse to remain offended,'" Grandma had once told me, quoting Galatians. "'We shall reap if we do not lose heart.'"

"The sooner we get started, the sooner we can start healing," I said.

Greg paused. "Well, I'm going to have to discuss with the team how we want to handle you," he said, and then got off. Sunil and Dan remained on the line.

"Hope, you did a good job," Dan said. "You said what you needed to say but in a respectful way. Hang in there."

His words encouraged me.

I flew to St. Louis on Thursday, October 12, two days before the game with Mexico.

By the time I reached the team hotel, it was late on Thursday night. I touched base with our general manager, Cheryl Bailey. She told me there would be a team meeting in the morning and gave me some words of advice. "One smile at a time," she said. "One hello at a time. You put your hand out, and even if no one takes it, you keep on trying."

I checked into my room. I was rooming with Tina. I couldn't help but remember that she had never spoken up for me in China. But I could tell she wanted to make things better between us.

"Hope," she said. "Guess what? I'm pregnant."

That was her gift to me, her olive branch—I was one of the first people she shared her news with. I hugged her.

At ten a.m. the next morning I went downstairs to a conference room. The chairs were arranged in a circle, and my teammates were already seated. There was an open chair next to Carli. I sat down. I was so nervous that I was shaking. I didn't want to see any of these women. Carli reached over and patted me on the leg. Everyone saw her do it.

Greg spoke first. "Hope, I know it takes courage for you to be here," he said.

Well, I thought, *that's a good start.* But then Greg recited a laundry list of my offenses. "We can't move forward until everyone gets out their feelings about what you did," he said. "All their feelings."

Each person stood up as they spoke.

Lil, the captain, started. She accused me of throwing the team under the bus. Then the rest followed.

"We don't think you should be here. We think you should go home."

"You're a bad friend."

"You're a terrible teammate."

"You threw us all under the bus."

"You just kept using your dad's death for sympathy."

That last jab was from Cat, my good friend. That hurt more than anything anyone else said.

When it looked like they were done, I started to speak. "I—"

"Are you even sorry?" someone interrupted. "You've never once been sincere."

"I can't stand this," Carli said, and left the room. I put my head down as Cat accused me of planning my statement to the press.

Aly, my other closest friend on the team, remained silent but had a cold look in her eyes. Tina looked miserable but didn't say anything.

I started rocking back and forth in my chair. I fought back tears. Carli came back into the room and sat back down beside me. "Stay strong, Hope," she whispered to me, and patted my leg. "Stay strong."

One of Greg's assistant coaches, Brett Hall, who had coached with Greg for years, finally spoke up. "Look, we all make mistakes," he said. "You have to pick that person up and move on as a team. You can't continue to make it worse; you want to forgive and move on."

His words hung heavily in the air. Greg shot him an angry look.

Finally, the meeting was adjourned. The message was clear: My teammates wished I had never shown up. Now they wanted me to go home, to make them look and feel better. The image of U.S. Soccer had taken an enormous hit. The once beloved team was being called Mean Girls.

The meeting had gone on so long that the team was late for training.

Greg told reporters that he had "excused" my

absence that day, as though it had been my choice to skip the workout.

At three p.m. I met with Cheryl and Dan Flynn. Dan was not happy when he learned what had happened. He told me to stay strong and not go home. "You're the future of the team," he said. "If I know the kind of person you are, you're going to prove them all wrong and come back and be the best goalkeeper in the game. Just stay patient."

The next morning I met with Greg. I had a sense he had been told by U.S. Soccer that he couldn't send me home. But he was determined to make it miserable for me. "The team doesn't want you here," he said. "They don't want you to sit on the bench."

"Well, I want to be here," I said. "I'm going to sit on the bench."

While the team warmed up for its first game, I stood on the field awkwardly. I was wearing jeans and tennis shoes, which seemed weird. Signs were held aloft in the stands: FREE HOPE SOLO and HOPE APOLOGIZED, THE TEAM OSTRACIZED. I heard some people chanting my name.

As I sat on the bench, Carli was the only player who would sit near me. Though the public was being told that our team was moving forward, no one looked in my direction. When my teammates came off the field, I reached out—as everyone on the bench does—to give high fives. A few of my teammates touched my hand, but most avoided me.

After the game, the team signed autographs, but I was hurried onto the bus. As my teammates filed on, they ignored me. Except for Christie Rampone, who paused at my seat and said, "How are you doing?"

"Okay," I said, my eyes starting to well. Her tiny bit of kindness almost burst me open.

Back at the team hotel, everyone exited the bus and headed to the elevator. I walked onto an elevator that was already carrying several of my teammates. After I stepped through the doors, my teammates got off. "I'm not getting on with her," Natasha Kai said loudly.

As the elevator doors closed, I burst out laughing. On my ride up to my room, a dam between pain and humor broke. This had become ridiculous.

When we got to Portland, the Nike athletes were invited to go to the Niketown store for a shopping spree. I was worried about my livelihood, but my friends at Nike were supportive. Stacey Chapman, one of the company's top marketing executives, hugged me when she saw me. She had been in China and witnessed how I had been treated, reporting back to Lesle how horrible the situation was. "Fake it till you make it," she said. "Keep smiling."

My mood improved dramatically in Portland. I was

in my Northwest comfort zone. My family and friends came to the game. On the field, I juggled the ball and goofed around; after the game, I defied the rules prohibiting me from signing autographs and went into the stands and embraced fans who had offered their support. I went out with my grandparents and Malia and her brothers after the game.

By the time we got to Albuquerque, I was feeling better. I had a meeting with assistant coach Brett Hall at a Starbucks. Brett was a tough guy, a demanding coach, but he had a forgiving heart. He told me that I was in a bad situation but I could learn from it. He said he thought hard times could mold greatness. "If you have to go through this, at least get something out of it," he said.

In the finale of the "celebration tour," we tied Mexico 1–1. After the game, Greg asked me to meet him on the second floor of the hotel outside the conference rooms. He sat at one end of the long table. I sat down at the other. "Here," he said, and slid something across the table toward me.

I caught it just before it dropped off the end of the table. It was my World Cup bronze medal, in a tiny Ziploc bag. This was my medal ceremony.

"Thank you for your services," he said, and shook my hand. Then he turned and went down the escalator, to where Sunil and Dan were waiting for him.

It was over. The tour, the season, the year. This team would never be same.

The next morning on the bus, everyone was hugging each other good-bye. Hugging everyone but me.

I flew home. When I landed in Seattle and turned on my phone, I had a message from Cheryl Bailey. "Hope," she said, "I wanted you to know that Greg has been fired."

16

THE NEW #1

GREG RYAN WAS GONE, BUT that didn't mean my problems were over. Three years earlier, I hadn't thought a head coaching change was a big deal. I believed talent won out. I was much wiser now.

The search committee was Mia Hamm, Dan Flynn, and Sunil Gulati. I figured Mia would look for a coach who would support the veterans, one who would take the side of Lil and Abby. Could any candidate possibly have an open mind about me? I wasn't sure of anything these days. As I waited in my cabin in Kirkland to find out who would be named coach, I read through the mail and email that had piled up since the World Cup.

In my mail, I found a small card with a Colorado postmark. It was from Greg Ryan. He wrote that to err is human and to forgive is divine. He added that we all make mistakes and need to forgive and that he hoped that would happen with me and my teammates. It seemed to be an odd time to say I needed to receive forgiveness. I had to wonder if his words were also a plea for himself.

The pick for new coach of the national team was Pia Sundhage. Pia was a pioneer of the women's game. For two decades she had played in Sweden, leading her country to World Cups in 1991 and 1995. After coaching in Sweden, she came to the WUSA as an assistant in Philadelphia. I had heard a lot of good things about her, but by the time I was drafted by Philadelphia, she had become Boston's head coach. Both Lil and Kate Markgraf played for her with the Breakers, and Pia had been the veterans' first choice to take over after April was fired. Those were red flags for me, but I had gotten to know Pia in Athens, where we shared housing and trained and even went out and had fun together. I liked her—I thought she was funny and interesting, and I was told she was a great coach.

Cheryl sent me the schedule of the upcoming

training camp. She told me that Pia had been told in detail about the past two months of turmoil. Two weeks before Christmas, we gathered in Southern California for a four-day camp to meet Pia. Bri was there, and so was Nicole Barnhart. I didn't know where I fit in—or if I fit in anywhere.

I walked into the hotel and saw my teammates embracing one another, excited to be reunited, squealing and laughing. But they got quiet as I walked down the hall to my room. No one greeted or hugged me.

I was still invisible.

We had our first team meeting. Pia talked a little bit about the schedule going forward, her plan and philosophy. Then she pulled out her guitar, explaining that English wasn't her native language and that she would sing us a song.

She started to strum her guitar and sing. Our new coach was singing Bob Dylan's anthem of transition. We listened in amazement as she finished up with the main chorus:

For the times they are a-changin'.

I smiled. I loved it.

Then Pia asked us, "Do you want to win?"

"Yes!" came the loud response.

"Well, to win you need a goalkeeper," Pia said. "I don't expect you to forget. But I do expect you to forgive. The Olympics are right around the corner, so let's get to work."

Meeting adjourned.

I felt bad on the field. I knew I wasn't playing well, that my lack of comfort and confidence was showing every day in practice. Pia came up to me during every practice to check on me. "How are you doing today?" she'd say.

"I'm okay, Pia," I'd tell her.

During the four-day camp, Pia met with many players and heard many sides to the story. She listened. She observed. She saw how isolated I was. Toward the end of camp, she sat down with me and asked questions. "I don't know what happened, and I don't know if I want to know what happened," she told me. "But in the end, we move on. I'm not making the choice for you. You have to make the choice whether you're on board."

I didn't have much to say. She could see for herself how I was struggling.

"I want you to trust me, Hope," she said. "Let's look forward instead of back."

The team came back together in early January to

prepare for the Four Nations Tournament in China. Word was out that Lil was pregnant with her first child and would miss the entire year, including the Beijing Olympics. That meant that the last of the '99ers was gone, at least for the immediate future. I was happy Lil was moving on with her life. But her absence also meant a major hurdle had just been removed from my path.

But even without Lil, the veterans were still trying to control our new coach. I found out through the grapevine that several veterans—even ones who were no longer on the team—had told Pia I wasn't ready to play, that I needed to learn how to sit on the bench and be a team player. But I was learning to trust my new coach. Pia seemed like someone who made her own decisions. She was looking at the big picture, thinking about who she would need in Beijing in August.

Pia named me to the Four Nations roster, and in China I started two out of three games. (Bri got the other game.) Even though I didn't feel I had earned the starts, I played well enough.

Pia started bringing in new young players like Tobin Heath and Lauren Cheney. They didn't share our recent tortured history; they had fresh eyes and attitudes. Pearcie had taken over the captain's armband from Lil. She was a confident, thoughtful leader; I remembered that on the celebration tour, she had been the only veteran to stop and speak to me. She didn't just talk about leadership; she showed it.

A few weeks after we won the Four Nations, we headed to Portugal for the Algarve Cup. Bri was left off the roster—Barnie and I split the four games. We played well, and for the first time in almost a year, I felt relaxed and happy. Maybe it was the mild Portuguese weather and the beautiful surroundings. Maybe it was because the veterans' circle had shrunk in size and power. Everyone seemed to be in a good mood. After we won, we all went dancing, Pia included.

Between the World Cup and the Olympics, there wasn't time to dwell on hurt feelings. The schedule was full: After Portugal we headed to Mexico to qualify for the Olympics, which we did with three wins and a tie.

After our trip to Mexico, we had a handful of friendly games in the United States: two with Australia, in North Carolina and Alabama, and another with Canada in Washington, DC. At those games, I took some abuse from Scurry fans. I heard boos behind the goal, and heckling.

"You're no Scurry."

"You'll never be as good as Bri. You suck, Solo."

"Get off the field."

I pretended that I didn't hear them.

As we edged closer to the Olympics, the press started to pay more attention to the team. How, reporters wondered, could this broken team heal? They started asking hard questions, ripping off the Band-Aid and seeing what was underneath. In Washington, DC, Grant Wahl from *Sports Illustrated* sat down with both Bri and me separately and asked us to revisit the details of 2007.

"I guess *Sports Illustrated* is doing a story," I said to Bri later.

"Yeah," she said.

We decided we should talk. For eight months, I'd been dreading this conversation, but at a café near our hotel, Bri and I talked for more than two hours. There was no anger. I apologized again, and she said she forgave me. We spoke of our fathers. Bri told me she had always thought I was a good kid before the World Cup. "I still think you're a good kid," she said.

We hugged. The scar was always going to be there, on both our careers. But the wound seemed to have finally healed.

When the Olympic roster was named in June,

Barnie and I were the goalkeepers. Bri was the alternate. It was the first time she wasn't on the roster for a world championship since the 1991 World Cup. An era had ended, and I felt it was time to mark the start of a new one. I had worn number 18 since college, when I still hoped to be a field player. But that was so long ago—I was a goalkeeper now, one of the best in the world. Goalkeepers traditionally wear number 1. I knew that requesting the number 1 jersey now could be portrayed as me stabbing Bri in the back again, but I felt strongly that the number 1 jersey should be worn by the starting goalkeeper. It was soccer tradition. And it represented a fresh start.

Secure in my place on the team, I started to make plans for my loved ones to come to the Olympics. Asking anyone to make two trips to China in the space of one year was a big request, and I had already received so much support for the World Cup that I wasn't sure what to expect. I was grateful for the support I was receiving—my mom was coming and my grandparents were committed.

Marcus wasn't going to come, but he had the best reason of all to skip the Olympics. He and his fiancée, Debbie, had become parents of a baby boy in April. Johnny, born a few days after my father's birthday, was named for my father. His birth brought joy and a sense of renewal to all of us.

Our last game before the Olympics was against Brazil in San Diego. Brazil, as usual, had struggled between the major tournaments and had been the last team to qualify for the Olympics. It was a warm night in July, and the stadium was packed with enthusiastic fans. In the first half, Abby and Andréia Rosa went into a hard tackle, and Abby never got up. She was flat on the ground and lifted her head to signal to the bench for help. I had never seen Abby in that kind of pain—not even when she had her head split open against North Korea.

The game came to a stop. Pearcie ran over to Abby. The paramedics lifted Abby onto a stretcher and placed an Aircast on her leg. She was taken to the hospital while the game continued. We won the game 1–0, but everyone on the team was in shock.

We found out after the game that Abby had broken both her left tibia and fibula. That's exactly what Abby, completely lucid, had told Pearcie on the field.

Abby—our force, our scoring threat—was out of the Olympics. We were going to have to win without her. Abby and I still didn't have much of a relationship, but we had reached a kind of truce: We agreed to disagree about what had happened at the World Cup last year. We were both key to the team's success: the goal scorer and the goal stopper. I couldn't imagine our team without her.

A few days later, we boarded the plane headed for Beijing. We hadn't lost a game since Pia took over—our last loss was the World Cup game against Brazil. I looked around at my teammates. There was no Lil, no Abby. Bri was only there as an alternate. Cat wasn't there—she was injured. Tina was home with her new baby. We were a completely different team. The times had, indeed, changed.

It was August 6—two days before the opening ceremonies—and we were playing our first Olympic game against Norway in Qinhuangdao, a seaport east of Beijing.

I had never been more scared to play a soccer game.

I knew how many people wanted me to fail.

When I took the field, I had too much adrenaline rushing through me. In the first two minutes, I made a terrible decision. Lori Chalupny was marking the Norwegian captain and was in perfect position. I charged off my line and tried to punch the ball out, but I clocked Chups in the head instead. The goal was left untended, and a Norwegian player easily headed the ball into the empty net. Not only had I made an error, I had injured Chups—our best defender. She left the game with a concussion.

The mistake rattled me. Then a Norwegian forward brought the ball down into the box and blasted a shot past me. Now we were down 2–0. And that's the way the game stayed. I was furious with myself. I couldn't believe we had lost our very first game and that our entire Olympics were suddenly at risk, all because I had worried about what other people thought. *What am I doing?* I thought. *Why am I letting the critics get to me?*

I thought of my dad, how he had always ignored those who judged him.

No more worrying what the haters think, I told myself.

We stayed in Qinhuangdao and watched the extravagant opening ceremonies on TV, but I couldn't enjoy the spectacle. *We were already being ripped to shreds in the press. We could never win without Abby. The World Cup wounds couldn't heal. We weren't a unified team.* In the eyes of the American media, we were already eliminated, forever in the shadow of the '99 team.

But Pia stayed positive. She didn't let us get down about the Norway result, and when we played Japan on August 9, we came out determined and attacking. In the first half, Carli scored a goal, and I played much better. We won 1–0 and headed to Shenyang to play New Zealand. What seemed impossible a few days earlier—winning our group—was within our grasp, if we won our game big and Japan beat Norway. I knew I couldn't afford to let in a goal. We did our part, winning 4–0. At the end of the game we celebrated and then heard the score of the Japan game: the Japanese had beaten Norway 3–1.

Our celebration circle on the field was an especially joyous one. Just ten months after the bitterness that had ripped our team apart, we were back to playing resilient, tough, unified soccer. It felt good.

In the quarterfinals, we played Canada in Shanghai. Midway through the first half we were leading 1–0 when rain began to pour down and lightning flashed around the stadium. The match was delayed for an hour and a half because of lightning strikes.

When the game resumed, my old nemesis, Christine Sinclair, blasted a shot past my extended body to tie the game. It took eleven minutes of overtime before Tasha Kai scored on a diving header to put us in the semifinals, where we would meet Japan again.

Our manager handed me an envelope. "This is for you, Hope."

Inside was a letter from Abby. Back home in upstate New York, she was rehabilitating, watching us and reflecting on the team. She had thought about coming to China but decided she would be a distraction. Instead, she wrote each of her teammates a letter. Even me.

She told me that she understood that as a goalkeeper I needed to have a strong belief in myself. She said that in the past year she'd learned to accept people for who they are. She said that she had tried to turn me into a villain for being myself.

"That isn't honest. That isn't compassionate. That is controlling and manipulative. I am sorry I was like that," Abby wrote. "You have a chance to show everyone who you really are. I believe you'll show everyone you're a winner."

I folded up the letter. I was blown away by the thought and feeling Abby had put into it. She could have written a perfunctory "Go for the gold!" but she had truly thought about our relationship and what was at stake. I was humbled and inspired. She had reached out across the ravine that separated us, and I knew I would grasp her hand. We didn't have to be best friends, but we had to be teammates. We needed each other.

Finally, after our quarterfinal, we traveled to Beijing, where all the other Olympic action was happening, and moved into the Olympic Village. We had never lost to Japan, but we knew how dangerous the Japanese were.

When our semifinal began, Japan jumped out in front in the first half, scoring on a corner kick. We tied the game late in the first half on a score that I started with a long goal kick. Just before the half we scored again and never relinquished the lead. The final score was 4–2.

I had played fine for the first five games of the tournament, but I hadn't been required to be a game-changer. In every major tournament, a team needs its goalkeeper to come up huge in at least one game, and that hadn't happened yet. The game hadn't called my name. But I would be ready when it did. We were in the gold-medal game. And our opponent was Brazil.

As we pulled up to Workers Stadium on August 21, I looked over at Carli. She smiled. "Here we go," I said.

"Here we go," she said.

Brazil's stars, Cristiane and Marta, were determined from the start to pick up where they'd left off in the World Cup, firing shot after shot at me. I dove to smother shots, punched balls out, collided with players. The game was calling my name.

In the seventy-second minute, Marta got behind two of our defenders and into the six-yard box. She shot at me from point-blank range. As she came at me, I read that she would hit the ball left to the far post, but she quickly changed and blasted the ball to my right. I had to react instantaneously, throwing up my arm to block the rocket shot, which felt like it would take off my arm. The force of the blow was so loud some observers thought the ball had struck the post. No, it had struck me, ricocheting out of danger. Marta thrust her hands up in frustration.

Regulation time ended in a 0–0 draw. We would play two fifteen-minute halves of overtime. Six minutes into overtime, Carli had a give-and-go with Amy Rodriguez and blasted a left-footed shot from the top of the box. It landed in the corner of the goal. We led 1–0.

"Oh yeah!" I said, pumping my fist at the far end of the field. But I knew we still had twenty-four minutes to play. Brazil was confident and relentless.

Marta beat our defense again and sailed a ball past me, just over the crossbar. Time seemed to have stopped, stretching out into the muggy Chinese night. Ball after ball was slotted through without anyone touching them. I pushed balls out with my fingertips, with one hand. We had been playing forever, an eternal battle, and still the whistle didn't come. As the seconds ticked down, Brazil earned corner after corner. Finally I saw the referee glance at his watch. It had to be time.

Renata Costa lofted another corner. Cristiane got her head on it. I made the save.

And then the whistle blew.

17

PRETTY SWEET

I SPRINTED OUT OF THE goal toward Carli and threw my arms around her.

My teammates and I collapsed onto one another, a jumble of cleats and tears and joy and sweat.

This was a celebration I'd been waiting for my entire life. We had our gold medal.

We had done it.

There was someone else I needed to share the moment with, someone who was back home in Washington, cradling his infant son, Johnny. Only Marcus really knew how shattered and vulnerable I had been at the World Cup. Before this game, I felt sure I would need to talk to him, so I had wrapped my cell phone in a white towel and placed it with my water bottle next to the goal. Marcus's number was predialed. I ran back to the goal from the celebration, retrieved my phone, and punched send.

"We just won the gold medal!" I shouted into the phone over the noise. "We did it!"

We did it. My teammates and I. Marcus and I.

"Yes!" he shouted back. "I'm so proud of you, Hope."

We were both laughing and crying, barely able to hear each other over the noise. "This is for Dad," he said over and over.

In my white towel, I had also placed a giant plastic gold medal—a ridiculous made-in-China prop that my mom and I had found in a Beijing marketplace. I put it on and ran over to where my family sat. My mom laughed in delight at my silly medal. My teammates and I reached up to the stands for high fives and hugs. Pearcie's daughter was passed down to her. American flags were handed down, and some of my teammates ran around the stadium wrapped in them. Everyone was celebrating.

When the podium was finally set up on the field for the medal ceremony, we put on our white jackets, specifically made for the gold-medal ceremony. As we lined up to step up on the podium, Bri came up to me and nodded. We hugged.

When I bowed my head and felt the medal slip around my neck, I heard the anthem play and saw my grandma with her red, white, and blue sweater and blinking HOPE NO. 1 sign pinned above her heart, singing at the top of her lungs. My grandpa was beaming with pride. My mother looked at me with so much love and amazement. They all shared this medal with me.

I thought of that moment years ago at the Sea-Tac Airport and how proud my dad had been when I won the gold medal in the Pan-American Games: He stopped strangers to tell them about how great his daughter was. I imagined how much he would have loved to see the gold medal hanging from my neck right now.

The team went back into the locker room and showered, and I stared at my medal for a very long time. I couldn't find my gloves, which were covered with writing: my dad's initials, words of inspiration from my grandma. I went back out to the field to look for them, but they were gone, probably snagged by some photographer looking for a souvenir.

When I came through the mixed zone on the way to the bus, there was a mob of reporters waiting for me, pressed up against the metal barricades, shouting questions about redemption and Greg Ryan. I had just won an Olympic gold medal. I wasn't thinking about the past, not about failures or hurts, and certainly not about Greg. This was my happiest moment. I was not going to let the devil steal my joy.

"How," someone asked, "does the moment feel?"

"It's unreal to me," I said. "It's like a storybook ending. It's something you see in Hollywood, a fairy tale, and yet it was playing out. And my life doesn't play out that way all the time, you know? There have been a lot of hardships. I was just hoping this one time it would really come through."

The thing about happy endings is, they don't last very long. In the early morning hours of October 31, my phone rang. It was Adrian. He needed me the way I had needed him sixteen months earlier. His dad, Bob Galaviz, had been over at his home the evening before. That night he gave Adrian an extra-long, tight hug before he walked out to his car. Driving south on Interstate 5, he'd been hit by a car. Bob was fifty-five years old.

I was in Richmond, Virginia, when I heard the news. We were going to play South Korea, still on our victory tour.

"Hope, I need you."

I told Pia I had to leave the tour.

18

UNPROFESSIONAL PROFESSIONALS

THE AIR WAS ICY. I shivered as I glanced over at Kristine Lilly. We were standing on a New York City sidewalk on the *Today* show to promote the launch of the WPS, our new professional league.

We took the same car service to the set and didn't speak a word to each other. Matt Lauer tried to put a soccer ball under Kristine's belly to illustrate how pregnant she had been a few months earlier. Meredith Vieira asked about the 2008 Olympic gold-medal performance. "It's been quite a year," I said, thinking back to the hardships I had been through just twelve months before. "It's a perfect time to kick-start a new league."

It was exciting to be involved in the launch of the first women's soccer league since WUSA. I would be playing for St. Louis.

But it wasn't the launch of the WPS that was the most important thing to happen to my soccer career in 2009. It was the arrival of Paul Rogers in my life. A really great goalkeeper coach is a rarity: I knew because I'd had dozens of them by then. Paul was English, arrogant, confident, demanding. I loved him. He immediately told me I sucked. He told Nicole Barnhart the same thing. *Who is this guy?* I thought, looking at Barnie.

And then Paul set about correcting our bad habits. We broke down film—not just game footage but film of practice. We examined tiny technical details like our balance, our first steps, the weight distribution in our feet, how far out our elbows were. It was the kind of complex examination I'd never been exposed to before.

Barnie and I could see all our faults, right there on film. It wasn't pleasant. *Wow!* I thought. *We really* do *suck.*

But then Paul set about building us back up. I knew there was so much more I could do, and I had finally found the coach who could take my work ethic and desire for instruction and push me harder than I had ever been pushed.

In that first tournament with Paul, I had three shutouts in the Algarve Cup and was named the MVP. Later, when I was named U.S. Soccer female Player of the Year for 2009, I made sure that I thanked Paul "for helping me think about the position in a more sophisticated way, both technically and tactically."

My fears about the solvency of the new WPS league were well-founded. Some of the same economic problems that had shut down the WUSA years earlier were still present in women's soccer.

Just a few weeks into my second season in St. Louis, the team's owner called a meeting. His business partners could not fund the team through the season. As of June 1, 2010, we were all free agents. I immediately signed with the Atlanta Beat, as did Tina, Chups, Kia McNeill, Aya Miyama, and a few of our other players. But I played only one game with Atlanta before leaving the country to go to the men's World Cup in South Africa.

Kia and I traveled with Team Up, a program affiliated with the Right to Play organization, reaching out to young people in the slums of Soweto, using soccer as a bridge for HIV-prevention education. We went to villages, met kids, and played soccer with them. I loved laughing and joking with them as they tried to get a shot past me. I was overwhelmed by their excitement at receiving a simple T-shirt or one of the braided bracelets I'd brought to give away. I was inspired by these children who were so knowledgeable about HIV and prevention and so determined to make a difference in their communities.

I had never been to a men's World Cup. The atmosphere was unbelievable—I enjoyed meeting the locals, blowing the *vuvuzelas* (plastic horns), experiencing the international excitement. I saw why the World Cup was often called the world's best sporting event, and I swore I'd never miss another.

But the games were only the second-best part of my trip. I've traveled the world playing soccer, but those moments with kids on the dirt fields in Soweto were among the most profound experiences I've ever had. I asked the kids what they wanted to do when they grew up. Their dreams were very real and specific. But one little girl said, "I don't have any dreams."

I hugged her. She broke my heart. By the end of our interaction, she told me that she did have a dream. "To teach everybody about AIDS," she said.

I was proud of her for dreaming to make a difference in the world.

When I got back to Atlanta, our team still hadn't won a game. I arrived in time to play in the All-Star Game in Atlanta. It was a fun day, but the league itself was facing serious troubles and was now in a state of desperation. It was clearly falling apart: Its commissioner had just been forced out, and several teams were on the brink of shutting down.

At the end of the season, I didn't know if there would be another one. But I had bigger concerns. I was now facing a new threat, one that could end my entire career. My right shoulder had been throbbing and aching for years, the result of more than a decade of abuse—hard landings on dives, bone-rattling contact with players and the turf. I was the Queen of Advil, but I refused to give in to the pain. After Portugal in 2009, I had an MRI because doctors suspected that I had a torn ligament in my elbow. It turned out I did have an injured elbow, but the doctor was most concerned about my shoulder. He said it was disintegrating, that there was nothing holding it together.

Surgery on my shoulder and elbow would mean that I would miss the 2011 World Cup. Even surgery on only my shoulder would still put me at risk of missing the World Cup. No surgery meant there was a chance that my shoulder would blow at any minute.

And the World Cup was just ten months away.

I talked to Pia. What would my status be if I had the surgery? I knew better than to assume that any starting position was written in stone. "Hope, you're leaving as our starting goalkeeper and you'll come back as our starting goalkeeper," Pia told me. "When you're medically cleared to play, you'll be our starter."

On September 21, I met with Dr. James Andrews, the world-renowned orthopedic surgeon, in Atlanta.

First, he did a physical strength test. "You're fine, kiddo," he said.

I was surprised. Then he went to his computer and looked at the images. The muscles around my shoulder were so strong that Dr. Andrews had been fooled into thinking the shoulder was functional. In truth, the muscles were the only things holding the joint together. "Can you be here at six a.m. tomorrow?" Dr. Andrews asked.

The decision was made for me. I was having surgery.

19

SEATTLE'S FINEST

WHEN I COULD FINALLY OPEN my eyes, I tried to take inventory. I was alone—in a hospital bed, my right shoulder bandaged and immobile, my head hazy from a potent dose of painkillers.

Dr. Andrews came in to see me. "The surgery took a very long time," he said. "It was extremely complicated." He had expected a ninety-minute operation. It had taken three and a half hours. Dr. Andrews told me he'd found extensive damage.

I tried to absorb everything he was telling me, but only one thing registered: My shoulder had been wrecked. And my return to soccer was in jeopardy.

"Hello?"

I snapped awake. Two young men were in my room, ready to take me down to rehab.

"Already?"

Yes, already. I was trying to condense a twelve-to-eighteen-month rehab into six months. I had to get back for the World Cup. I had to start rehab immediately.

I was miserable, but there was nothing I could do. I wanted to hide from the other patients, so I asked them to put my sunglasses on my face. Then they put me in a wheelchair and wheeled me down to the rehab clinic—every bump and turn on the journey causing me to grimace in pain.

That first morning, the therapist took my arm out of the sling and had me straighten it. That was all I had to do. I thought I was going to die. A Tampa Bay Rays pitcher who'd had shoulder surgery four months earlier was in the clinic working out; he looked at me with deep sympathy. "I don't miss those days," he said.

I never took off my sunglasses. I didn't want anyone to see the tears in my eyes.

After a couple of weeks I left Alabama. I went to Atlanta to pack up my belongings and headed back to Seattle, where my mom stayed with me. She saw to my every need and drove me an hour each way to my physical therapy.

I tracked the qualifying games online. The first three games were lopsided victories over Haiti, Guatemala, and Costa Rica. But on November 5, our team lost to Mexico 2–1. It was our first-ever loss to Mexico, and it put our backs against the wall: We had to beat Costa Rica in a third-place match in Cancún and then play a home-and-home with Italy for the right to play in the World Cup.

The team's struggles only added to my misery. I could barely move my arm two inches to the side. I couldn't raise it at all. It was hard to imagine playing in the World Cup in just a few months. That is, if our team made it to the World Cup.

On November 20, I woke up early to track the game in Italy. It was agonizing, almost as bad as the rehab session that awaited me later in the day. Our team couldn't score, and the game went into extra time. Finally in the ninety-fourth minute, our youngest team member, Alex Morgan—who had just finished her senior year at Cal—pushed a shot past the diving Italian goalkeeper for a 1–0 victory. We still had life.

It was torture watching from afar, unable to do anything to help. I decided to meet my team in Illinois for the final do-or-die game against Italy. Everyone was a little shocked to see the shape I was in. I had lost weight, and my arm had completely atrophied from lack of exercise.

"You need to gain some muscle," Pia said.

"I'm trying," I said.

The game was tense, but in the end we won 1–0. We were going to Germany next summer. But who would be the starting goalkeeper?

Snap. Crackle. Pop. Moan.

My shoulder sounded like a bowl of cereal as my therapists helped me stretch through my pain to break up the scar tissue. They pushed me all winter. Sometimes our sessions lasted six hours. Pain and suffering was my full-time job.

The team went to China in January, but I wasn't ready to travel with them—again I watched online. The results were mixed: We lost in our first game to Sweden. Though we won two other games, we didn't dominate in any of them.

In March, I was medically cleared to join the team, so I joined them in camp for the Algarve Cup. I could sense tension—a vibe that seemed very familiar. The World Cup was just three months away and Pia, like Greg four years earlier, was starting to stress out. She hadn't faced much pressure until now. When she took over before the '08 Olympics, she had inherited a damaged, dysfunctional team. Getting to the gold-medal game eight months later was a bonus. But she'd guided the top-ranked team in the world for three years now. The players were the ones she had chosen. The team was struggling, and it didn't help that her starting goalkeeper could barely move.

I was mentally ready to get back to work, but I was weak physically. I started simply, working on my footwork. Everything that had once been so easy for me was difficult. I got frustrated and started to lose confidence. I had been so impatient in rehab, where that mind-set worked for me, but on the field I had to learn to be patient. Paul wouldn't let me face a shot until we got to Portugal. There, he tossed balls to me. I was scared to react, so fearful of the pain. Every time I touched the ball, I was in pain. The first time I dove, I thought my shoulder anchors would rip loose. *If I can't do this,* I thought, grimacing from a soft-tossed ball, *how the hell am I going to stop Abby's shots?*

I looked into Paul's eyes to see if I could spot doubt, but I didn't. He never questioned me. Instead, he guided me in baby steps. Four shots to each side of my body one day, five shots the next. A little bit more confidence every day. He was protective and patient—creating drills in conjunction with my therapists that would increase both my range of motion and my healing. "You're going to have pain," Paul said, "so you're going to have to learn to manage it."

We were in London to play a friendly against England. At long last, I was medically cleared to play. We were six months past my surgery, eleven weeks away from the World Cup opener. I needed to start—I was running out of time. I'd been working toward game day, April 2—my dad's birthday—for months as my target goal. Pia had already announced her starting lineup at practice, and I was in it. I was excited. Now, Paul was delivering some difficult news. "You're not starting," he told me.

"We only have four games left before the World Cup," I said. "I need time to prepare."

"You'll get the second half," Paul said. When I protested, he asked, "Do you think you beat out Barnie?"

"Hell no, I haven't beat out Barnie," I said. "She's playing the best I've ever seen her. But you and Pia have said you want me to be your starting goalkeeper for the World Cup, and I need to get games. I need to fail, to make mistakes now so that I don't make them closer to the World Cup. Now you're only giving me three and a half games to get ready for our most important tournament."

But Paul didn't think I was ready. It was the biggest argument he and I had ever had. I knew he didn't want to wreck my confidence, but I needed as many minutes as possible after sitting out for six months. I had been following a plan we had laid out back in September, and now the plan was changing.

I felt I had done my part, and I trusted my coaches to uphold their end.

Paul told me to clean myself up and go meet with Pia. She took one look at my face and knew I was upset. "What are you feeling?" she said.

I told her that I needed every minute I could get and that she was taking a crucial forty-five minutes away from me.

"You don't think you can be ready in three and a half games? You need these forty-five minutes to be ready for the World Cup?"

I could hear the doubt in her voice. Pia was losing faith in me.

"Pia, I'll be ready for the World Cup if you only give me two games. I'll do whatever it takes. But you know as well as I do that every minute counts."

"Get yourself ready to play in the second half then," she said, dismissing me.

I'm going to prove to her that I'm ready, I thought.

I entered the game in the second half, my first live action since my last game of the WPS season. We were down 2–1 when I came in. We hadn't played very well in the first half, and Barnie had seen a ton of action. I didn't see much action at all, which was irritating. I needed to make some tough decisions, get challenged in traffic. Still, it felt great to get back on the field. Paul was pleased—nothing had happened to damage the most important part of my game, my confidence. But our team lost the game, our first loss ever to England.

What, the media started to wonder, was wrong with the U.S. national team?

The WPS was still going. Sort of. Investors were dropping out, teams were folding, and the league was down to just five teams now. It was a slow death march.

I had signed with a team called the MagicJack. The Washington Freedom franchise had been purchased by the inventor of the MagicJack phone technology, Dan Borislow, and he moved the team to his hometown of Boca Raton, renamed it for his company, and signed a bunch of national team players.

Dan did things his way. The league hated that he was using the team to promote his company and that he wouldn't abide by league rules.

I made my first start for the MagicJack on May 1. I was happy to be playing in the WPS this time. It was good to get some more games under my belt, and a bunch of the national team players, including Abby and Pearcie, were also playing for the MagicJack.

But the experience was bizarre. The MagicJack coach quit after the team won its first three games, so our team was coached by Pearcie and Dan. It was strange but really not all that much of a departure from the screwball behavior that had marked the league's entire existence. And I was too focused on my shoulder and the World Cup to worry about the WPS too.

On May 14, I finally got my first national team start in Columbus against Japan. Mentally I was ready, but my arm felt terrible. But at least I was tested—I had a good tip-over save and some tough balls on set pieces. We beat Japan 2–0 that day and by the same score four days later in North Carolina.

As we counted down the days to the World Cup, I got a call from my one of my dad's old friends. "Hope, did you know the murder of Mike Emert has been solved?" he said. "Did you know your father is no longer a suspect?"

And then he told me a story straight out of *CSI*. In the fall of 2010, Mike Emert's widow, Mary Beth, was told there was a DNA match—they had found her husband's killer. But the killer was now dead. A retired Seattle cop named Gary Krueger had been involved in a home invasion in March 2010. Krueger tried to force his way into the upscale home of an orthopedic surgeon; when the police were called, Krueger fled, stole a boat in Lake Washington, and capsized it. His body wasn't pulled out of the lake until September. At that time, his DNA was put into a database and came up as a solid match for DNA found at the Emert crime scene: skin under Emert's fingernails and blood in his stolen SUV.

I was stunned. We had never even been told there was any DNA at the scene that could have cleared my father. But that wasn't the end of the story. Krueger had been a rogue cop in the late 1970s. After he retired in 1980, he turned to criminal schemes and was a suspect in a couple of murders, including Emert's. Krueger was finally convicted for a series of bank robberies and went to prison, where his DNA should have been collected and entered into the database. But it wasn't collected until he was released on parole in 2007, and then it was never entered into the database. There was no explanation for the three-and-a-half-year delay. Marcus had made some phone calls. One of his sources in the police department told him that it was clear that my father had been framed. Krueger had intentionally dressed like him, adopted a New York accent and a limp, and arranged to meet Emert at a place where my dad hung out.

20

IT JUST TAKES ONE

AFTER TEN DAYS IN A beautiful alpine spa, our national team boarded a charter flight for Dresden. We were about to play our first game of the 2011 World Cup, against North Korea. At the airport, we were greeted by a World Cup official with a Team USA sign. We saw the World Cup banners in the airport. This was it.

The atmosphere in Germany was exhilarating. A few hours before the game on June 28, I got a huge shot of the painkiller Toradol. I knew what was going to happen next. My arm would feel like Gumby— bendable and able to do anything. And after the game, I was going to be in agony from moving my shoulder in ways I shouldn't have been able to. My shoulder was now my source of inspiration. Athletes have to keep finding new forms of motivation, and this was mine.

In 2007, I was motivated to play for my father's memory.

In 2008, I was playing not only for myself but also for my mom and Marcus, Grandma and Grandpa, Adrian, Mary and Dick, Lesle and Amy—my lifelong team.

In 2011, my motivation was the constant pain in my shoulder. I wanted to prove the doubters wrong, to show that I could come back from a devastating injury. And I wanted to earn the right to be called the best goalkeeper in the world.

I reminded myself to lock in every memory. I tried to soak in each moment—standing apart from my team during warm-ups to look at the faces in the crowd, to study my opponents, to enjoy the vibrant colors in the stadium. Not every athlete gets to experience such a grand event.

Though the game lacked the dramatics of 2007, it was far from easy. I had to make two difficult saves in a ten-minute span in the first half. There was no score at halftime, but early in the second half, Lauren Cheney headed in a perfect service from Abby.

Twenty minutes later, Rachel Buehler gathered up a deflection on a corner and scored. We won 2–0.

We flew to Frankfurt and then took a bus to Heidelberg, where we practiced in front of a group of American military personnel and their families. I felt so proud to be wearing a USA jersey. It was thrilling to get that kind of hometown support in a foreign country.

The sold-out crowd at Rhein-Neckar Arena two days later was full of American flags and red-white-and-blue painted fans. We dominated the Colombia team. Heather O'Reilly scored in the first half, and we all ran to one sideline and saluted the fans. (It was the first time I had ever celebrated a goal on the field.) In the second half, Megan Rapinoe and Carli added goals. When Megan scored, she ran to the oversized microphone in the corner of the field, picked it up, and sang "Born in the USA" as a tribute to all the Americans in the crowd. We were having fun. The 3–0 final assured us of a spot in the quarterfinals, even though we had one more game of group play— against our toughest opponent, Sweden.

The tournament was getting rave reviews. The stadiums were packed, the crowds were electric, and many of the games were thrillingly close. The competition was far more evenly matched than it had ever been before. It was stunning how much women's soccer had progressed around the globe. I could see it starting to happen when I had been playing overseas. Now teams that had never made an impact before, like France and Japan, were serious threats.

We flew to Wolfsburg, where it was raining. I could tell that Pia, though happy we had advanced, really wanted to beat Sweden, the team she had starred for as a player. But we had bad luck, and Sweden played smart and physical. In the first half, Amy LePeilbet took down my old buddy Lotta Schelin in the penalty box and was given a yellow card. I guessed right on the penalty kick and was fully extended, but the ball slipped just past my fingertips. Twenty minutes later, a free kick ricocheted off Amy's thigh and past me into the goal. We were down 2–0.

We had our chances but didn't score until Abby got us on the board in the second half. The 2–1 loss was our first ever in group play and meant we finished second in the group.

I wasn't stressed about that. We had lost in group play in the Olympics to Norway and won the gold medal. We had advanced. That was all I cared about. But we were taking a difficult path. Our quarterfinal opponent was Brazil.

The match felt epic from the start. The stadium was sold out, and the air crackled with the kind of electricity that only comes in big sporting events.

A lot was made of the fact that we were playing on the twelfth anniversary of the 1999 World Cup final. Many of the '99ers were in Germany working for ESPN: Brandi, Bri, Mia, and Julie, as well as Tony DiCicco.

Lesle and Amy and their kids had been in Germany for the entire tournament. The rest of my support group arrived in time for the Brazil match: my mom, Marcus and Debbie and little Johnny, my sister, Terry, Aunt Susie and Uncle Frank and their sons. And Adrian was there too. As the national anthem played, I spotted my loved ones in the stands. Unfortunately, my grandma and grandpa weren't there; Grandpa Pete had been diagnosed with dementia, and his health was declining. Grandma Alice didn't want to leave him.

We got on the board almost instantly. Brazilian defender Daiane scored an own goal trying to clear a ball Boxxy had sent in. It was the opposite of what had happened to us in 2007. It was a nice start, but we knew we were in for a long day. We clung to the 1–0 lead at halftime.

In the sixty-fifth minute, Marta came streaking toward me with Rachel Buehler chasing. Rachel made a slide tackle, taking Marta down in the penalty box—a player like Marta is always going to get that call. Rachel was shown a red card and, completely distraught, left the field. Once again we were going to be playing shorthanded against Brazil. Even worse, Cristiane was lining up against me to take the penalty kick. As I made my way into the goal, I was swinging my arms to loosen up my shoulder. I jumped up and down, raising my arms a few times, just to let Cristiane know I was there, and then I was set.

Cristiane shot to her right. I read correctly, diving to my left and batting the ball away. I was so fired up—saving a penalty kick takes both luck and skill and can be a huge momentum shifter. I jumped to my feet, clapping, and Carli and Boxxy ran up to hug me. But then mass confusion broke out—the referee had waved off the save and was awarding Brazil a do-over. She told me I had moved off my line. I was sure I hadn't; I never believed in moving off the line because I didn't feel it gave me any advantage on the read. The ref showed me a yellow card as I raised my hands in protest. "Are you kidding me?" I shouted.

The crowd started to turn right then, booing the referee and booing Brazil for getting an unfair advantage. As boos and whistles rained down on her, Marta stepped up to retake the shot Cristiane had missed. Of course, she made it this time. The game was tied 1–1, and we were shorthanded. Our team gathered to talk about setting the defense without

Rachel. Boxxy was going to move back, taking on more defensive responsibilities. I was still in shock over the bad call. As I went back to my line, I raised my hand again in disbelief. The crowd took it as a cue and began to chant, "USA! USA!" Brazil had tied the score but lost the home-field advantage.

Regulation ended in a tie: We would play two fifteen-minute overtime periods.

Two minutes into overtime, Marta got her left foot on a cross that I thought had come from a player who was offside. Boxxy raised her hand to signal offside, but no call was made. Marta lofted the ball toward the far post and into the net. Brazil was ahead 2–1 and had a man advantage. I didn't lose hope, but as the minutes passed and our shots flew wide or high, things were looking grim. I started to worry.

We were in the 122nd minute of the game. At my end of the field, Pearcie passed the ball to Ali Krieger. Krieger passed to Carli in the defensive end, who then beat two players and passed wide to Megan Rapinoe. She brought the ball down toward Brazil's goal and sent a hopeful twenty-five-yard cross off her left foot, perfectly placed toward the net. Abby launched herself toward the ball, hit it squarely with her forehead, and sent it screaming into the back of the net.

We all went crazy. Abby ran toward the sideline

and then slid on her knees; she was instantly dog-piled by her teammates. The fans exploded in a roar of amazement, and I was jumping up and down and wheeling my arms around, alone on my side of the field. I looked into the stands and spotted Adrian as I screamed with joy.

The whistle blew. We were going to penalty kicks.

My team was amped up at midfield, full of energy and adrenaline and pulsing with confidence. I walked away from them to compose myself; I didn't need amping up. I needed to be calm and clear-minded. I walked over to the corner flag on the side of the field where my loved ones were sitting.

"It just takes one," Amy said. I could see her mouth the words and hold up one finger. I was having my own private moment with the people who meant the most to me, in the midst of 25,000 people.

"It just takes one," Amy said again.

Okay, I thought. *I've got this.*

We had practiced penalty kicks the day before. I had a good feeling.

Boxxy went first for us. Andréia, Brazil's goalkeeper, came so far off her line to block the shot that even the unfair ref couldn't mess up the call. Boxxy retook the kick, went the same way—to her right—and made it easily.

U.S. 1, Brazil 0.

I stood up and windmilled my arms as I walked to the line. Cristiane was waiting. I didn't get a good read on the ball—she went to her left and made the shot. U.S. 1, Brazil 1.

Carli was up next. She hammered the ball into the left-side netting past a diving Andréia. U.S. 2, Brazil 1.

Marta walked up next as the crowd booed and whistled. The greatest player in the world had turned into the villain. I've always liked Marta—she plays with so much passion and soul. I guessed left, she went to my right. U.S. 2, Brazil 2.

Abby was next. She never even looked at Andréia. She kept her head down and put the ball in the right corner of the net. U.S. 3, Brazil 2.

Daiane walked up. I watched her line up to shoot. I felt confident.

I got a good read on the ball. I extended completely to my right and extended my hand, pushing the ball safely away. I was already celebrating as I landed; I rolled over and jumped up, my arms in the air in triumph. *It just takes one.* And I had one. U.S. 3, Brazil 2.

Rapinoe was next. She shot under a diving Andréia. U.S. 4, Brazil 2.

Franciela was up. She put a shot past my right hand. U.S. 4, Brazil 3.

One more converted kick and we would win,

completing the amazing comeback. I went back to my corner to watch.

Ali Krieger stepped up. She kept her head down and didn't look at Andréia, who stood on the line like the Cristo statue in Rio, arms outstretched. Andréia jumped off her line well before Ali shot, but it didn't matter. Ali tapped her shot into the left corner of the net. U.S. 5, Brazil 3.

Ali sprinted toward our bench, where the reserve players and coaches were flooding onto the field, leaping with joy. The players on the field all ran to envelop Ali.

All but one. Abby veered to her right, sprinting straight toward me. I ran to her and leaped into her arms, and we fell to the ground. Together.

21

THE SILVER LINING

FORTY-SEVEN THOUSAND FANS IN YANKEE Stadium roared at the big screen as we went to penalty kicks against Brazil. Flights in Denver were delayed until the game ended. Everyone back home, it seemed, had stopped whatever they were doing to watch our game as Sunday morning stretched into Sunday afternoon. Even if they didn't start out watching it, as the game progressed, someone called or tweeted or posted on Facebook about this amazing soccer game, and more and more people tuned in to see what it was all about. And they were captivated.

"I *love* these women!" tweeted Tom Hanks.

LeBron James offered, "Congrats, ladies!"

"Amazing game," Aaron Rodgers tweeted. "Now let's get the cup, ladies!"

I was named the player of the match. That night Abby and I took a car service to the ESPN set in downtown Dresden. "When did you score your goal?" I asked her in the back of the car while I checked the messages and texts flooding my phone.

"I think in the 120th minute," Abby said.

No, Aaron Heifetz said, it was later than that. It was the latest goal ever scored in the World Cup. The 122nd minute. "Oh my God," we both said.

"I don't get how that just happened," Abby said of the match. "I just kept saying, 'One chance.' That's all we need."

On the ESPN set, we finally had a chance to see the highlights, every crazy thing that happened in the game. We couldn't believe the roller coaster we had just been on. "Everything was against us," I told host Bob Ley. "This team has something special. We found a way to win."

It was inevitable that 2007 would come up. How, Ley asked, did we put the divisions behind us? Perhaps, he wondered, there were even tensions between the two of us? We both just smiled. "Pia came in and changed the dynamics of the team," I said. "And to be honest, we grew up. We threw our differences out the window and learned to respect one another off and on the field."

Abby said, "I'd rather have no other person in goal behind me; this woman saves sure goals. Hope's the best goalkeeper in the world."

Abby and I were on *Good Morning America* the next day. Some American journalists who hadn't been in Germany flew in to write stories about the most talked-about sports team on the planet. Everyone was calling the Brazil game the greatest moment for women's soccer since the 1999 World Cup, and the overnight television ratings were the best they'd been since that epic tournament.

Two days later, we played our semifinal game against France. It was my hundredth cap: one hundred games for the national team since that first one in the spring of 2000, when I played against Iceland as an eighteen-year-old college freshman.

Now I was two weeks away from my thirtieth birthday, my shoulder full of scar tissue and metal and pain. I was a veteran.

The night before the game, my goalkeeper coach, Paul, told me he wanted to go over film with him. To my surprise, after we sat down in front of the screen to watch video, all my teammates entered the room. Paul started the film: It was a compilation he had put together of almost every one of my hundred games. It was hilarious—different uniforms, my hair changing color as the years passed. My teammates applauded and laughed and gave me cards with their handwritten tributes. The compilation ended, of course, with the Brazil game. Everyone cheered. I was touched. It was a beautiful gift. It had taken me eleven long years to get to one hundred—only the second goalkeeper in U.S. history, along with Bri, to achieve that mark. It was worth the wait to earn the honor with this team. My team.

France was all over us on that rainy Wednesday night. We got an early goal on a cross from Lauren Cheney that Heather O'Reilly tapped in, but France was relentless, connecting passes and unafraid to shoot.

France tied the game in the second half, when I came out for a cross that Sonia Bompastor looped in toward a runner; I was expecting a header, but the runner leaped over the ball, and it slipped into the right side of the net. France continued to dominate possession. Alex Morgan came in for Amy Rodriguez immediately after France tied the game and was aggressive right away. She almost scored but was called offside on the play. Still France kept pushing forward; a shot at the World Cup final was twelve minutes away. And then Abby's forehead came to the rescue again. Lauren Cheney sent a corner to the far post and Abby rose up above everyone—I could see her elevate from my end of the field—and hammered the ball into the net.

Moments later Alex, our rookie, scored her first World Cup goal, lifting the ball over French goalkeeper Berangere Sapowicz, who had slipped to the ground, to give us a 3–1 lead. A few minutes later, the victory was complete. We were in the World Cup final for the first time since 1999.

We drove by bus to Frankfurt, the site of the final. We tried to recover our legs and relax a little. The pain in my shoulder was getting worse and worse, and I went through hours of treatment between games. On the practice field, I couldn't dive. I did everything I could to save myself for the competition. And every night I had to take a heavy dose of painkillers to get to sleep. I was taking a series of shots to prepare for games, something that needed to be scheduled and planned: cortisone, Synvisc, Toradol. Every time the long needle plunged deep into my joint, there was searing pain followed by brief relief.

We knew Japan well. We had played them three times in 2011. A lot was being made of our 22–0–3 record against them, but we had suffered our first losses to Mexico and to England in recent months, so we knew all streaks eventually end. Japan's history in the World Cup wasn't impressive: They had won only three games. But they finished fourth in the Beijing Olympics after losing to us in the semifinals, and they had continued to improve.

We also knew that they were playing at an emotional level that we couldn't comprehend. The wounds from the March 9.0 earthquake and devastating tsunami in Japan hadn't even begun to heal. The dead—upward of 15,000—were still being counted, and thousands more were missing. After the disaster, I tried for days to reach Aya, who was from one of the areas that suffered heavy damage. The country had rallied behind their gutsy women's team, which—playing on the other side of the world—was showing a new tenacity.

The night before the final, I received an email from Aya, wishing me luck. Normally, I would never respond to a message from an opponent, but I knew these were moments we would never get back. It felt right to honor a person I respected so much, who competed so hard.

Aya,
Let's enjoy this moment no matter what happens.
   Hope

Inside the stadium, 50,000 people greeted us, many of them holding signs and waving American flags.

There were several *Star Wars*–inspired tributes to me—HANDS SOLO and THE FORCE IS WITH YOU, SOLO. MARRY ME, HOPE, I'M SOLO. Eight fans held up giant letters spelling out my name. Some people wore replicas of my big white goalie gloves. Even President Barack Obama sent out a tweet to our team that morning: "Sorry I can't be there to see you play, but I'll be cheering you on from here. Let's go."

It felt like our day from the start. I had little to do early on and watched my teammates get chance after chance: Lauren Cheney, Rapinoe, Carli, Abby. But the shots went wide. They went high. Rapinoe hit the post. Abby hit the crossbar. We were dominating possession, but nothing was going in, and we were tied at halftime. Finally, in the sixty-ninth minute, Alex Morgan broke the drought. We were twenty minutes away from winning the World Cup. We needed to stay strong. But falling behind seemed to energize Japan. We had a defensive lapse, and my old pal Aya made us pay, pouncing on the ball directly in front of the goal and banging it past me to tie the game in the eightieth minute.

Nothing came easy in this World Cup. Regulation ended in a tie, and we headed to overtime. In the 104th minute, Alex sent a cross directly to Abby's forehead, and she slammed the ball in. We had a 2–1 lead in overtime with the World Cup on the line. But who knew better than us that teams can come back in overtime? Early in the second extra-time period, I collided with Yukari Kinga and cut my knee badly.

A few minutes later, we cleared the ball behind our goal, setting up a corner. Thirty-two-year-old Sawa redirected the kick, which glanced off Abby and into the net. Tied again. Twice Japan had fallen behind and faced elimination, and twice the team had rallied back. The momentum had shifted. Destiny seemed to have switched sides.

The game went to penalty kicks. Our long World Cup road was almost at an end. I knew how psychologically hard it was for a team to win two games in one tournament on penalty kicks. Japan had already seen us take kicks against Brazil just a week earlier; they had film to study. We didn't have that advantage.

It didn't go well from the start. Boxxy shot first, but Japan's goalkeeper, Ayumi Kaihori, made a kick save.

Aya made her penalty kick to put Japan up 1–0.

Carli sent her shot high over the crossbar.

I made a save on Yuki Nagasato, diving to my right.

Tobin Heath's shot was saved by Kaihori.

Mizuho Sakaguchi made her shot, and Japan had a 2–0 lead. One more converted penalty kick by Japan and the game would be over.

Abby made her penalty kick to cut it to 2–1.

Then Saki Kumagai sent the ball high over my right shoulder, above my outstretched hand. Japan won the World Cup.

They ran to one another as we watched in shock. They jumped and cried, and confetti poured from the rafters. They unfurled a sign, TO OUR FRIENDS AROUND THE WORLD—THANK YOU FOR YOUR SUPPORT. I walked over to the stands, as I always do, to where my friends and family sat. I wanted to see the love in their faces. We had done everything we could and played in an unforgettable World Cup. The feeling after the loss was so different than it had been in 2007; it was painful, but we weren't crushed. It was pain that came with an honest, honorable defeat. I then walked back to congratulate the Japanese players and hugged Aya. She wasn't celebrating. "I don't want to celebrate while you are hurting," she told me.

"Aya," I said, hugging her. "Please celebrate. You won the World Cup!"

As I started to leave the field, I was stopped for an interview. "As much as I've always wanted this," I said, my voice cracking, "if there was any other team I could give this to, it would have to be Japan."

Despite our loss, I knew that what had happened

was good for women's soccer. We had built up the game. We had rebuilt our team. I was so proud of everything that we had accomplished together, how far we had come.

22

FAIRY-TALE ENDING

I DIDN'T KNOW WHAT LAY ahead for me after the World Cup, but I knew one thing: I wasn't going back to the MagicJack. After pushing my shoulder so hard—ten months of grueling rehab and competition—I needed to take a long break from soccer. My goal for the 2012 Olympics was to be healthy and no longer reliant on the pain medication I had been taking for so many months.

When the team arrived in New York on the Monday after the final, we were greeted by television cameras, media requests, and a huge throng of enthusiastic fans waiting for us in Times Square. We appeared as a team on the *Today* show, where we were told that our final game broke a world record for "tweets per second"—surpassing even the royal wedding. We were overwhelmed by our new celebrity status and a bit confused. Only Pearcie—the last of the '99ers—had ever experienced anything like this. But that team had won the World Cup. We had played well, but we had lost.

That made the enthusiastic response even more moving: It was all about the game. Everyone was talking about women's soccer.

Then my agent called with an interesting proposal. Would I like to be one of the celebrity contestants on the show *Dancing with the Stars*? "Sure, that sounds fun," I told Rich with a laugh, not really taking it seriously. I knew my soccer schedule would be way too busy.

Then I took a closer look. The national team had only two games scheduled in a celebration tour. There might be one more friendly scheduled in the fall. But our run-up to Olympic qualifying wasn't going to get serious for a couple of months. I gulped. Turns out I *could* do *Dancing with the Stars*. A grubby kid from Richland all dressed up in sparkles in Hollywood, like Cinderella at the ball? A former tomboy in a wig, fake eyelashes, and spackled-on makeup?

Everyone tried to convince me: "It'll be a great showcase for women's soccer."

That was true. Besides, I'd always wanted to learn to dance.

I sat in a car next to a soccer field in Westchester, not far from the Los Angeles airport. The cameras were all set to capture the moment I met my *DWTS* partner, the pro I would rely on. I suspected that my partner was going to be Maksim Chmerkovskiy—the handsome "bad boy" of the show, who liked to keep his shirt unbuttoned. He was also the only pro dancer tall enough to pair with me.

A red Rolls-Royce pulled up to the soccer field, and Maks got out. I started laughing—what a Hollywood entrance. As my producers requested, I got out of my car and began warming up in goal, and they shot Maks walking across the field to meet me. It was so staged and awkward. I tried to keep it real and break the ice—I started giving Maks a hard time. "Wow, those are some tight jeans you're wearing," I said. And, "Are dancers even real athletes?"

When he assured me that he was very athletic, I said, "Come on, Maks—let's see how good you are at my profession. Block some of my shots."

I started shooting balls at him, and he shuffled back and forth in front of the goal as best he could in his tight jeans while I drilled balls past him.

Later that day, we had our first rehearsal.

I'm an athlete, I'm competitive, and I'm confident that I can excel at any physical activity, but dancing was harder than I expected.

The first show was September 19. On September 17, I started for the national team in a "celebration tour" game in Kansas City. Maks came with me—we had to find a dance studio near the hotel so we could practice. Though the scheduling was insane, it was great to be back on the field with my teammates. The normal routine helped ease my nerves and distracted me from what was looming in just a matter of hours.

The night of the first *DWTS* show, I was so scared I thought I might be sick. My support crew was there: Adrian, Terry, and Tina had all flown in. When I walked into the trailer that served as my home on the lot, they were shocked. "Hope, you've never looked so girly!" Tina said.

I was wearing a sparkling pink dress with flowing sleeves, long dangling earrings, and a necklace. I downed a glass of white wine to calm my nerves. "You're beautiful. You're going to be incredible," Adrian whispered in my ear as I left the trailer.

Maks and I waltzed to Dave Matthews's "Satellite." The good news: I didn't fall down, and I didn't make any major mistakes. When the song ended, I was exhilarated. I looked over at my section—my support group was giving me a standing ovation. And then the judges spoke. Though they were complimentary, each one mentioned my "strength" or my "muscles." I was told I needed to be more feminine, as though having muscles and being strong wasn't feminine. I smiled. I was relieved it was over, but I wasn't sure what they wanted from me.

It was starting to get strange to be in restaurants or other public places. The paparazzi started following me. People stood up and clapped when I walked into restaurants. Drinks were sent to the table. I appreciated the support, but it was unnerving.

The best part was all the support I got from my friends and family. Terry was so loving and involved— my sister, who used to love to dress me up and do my hair, was there for the ultimate game of dress-up. One week we danced the foxtrot to "You've Got a Friend in Me," from *Toy Story*, with Maks and me dressed up as Woody and Jessie. That week, Grandma Alice and Marcus came and brought Johnny, who was wearing his Buzz Lightyear Halloween costume.

During this crazy, hectic period, my relationship with Adrian was growing stronger every week. He came down from Seattle every Sunday and stayed until Thursday. He shopped and cooked for us and bolstered my confidence. I realized that for so many years, we had been performing our own strange dance—back and forth, pushing away and pulling back. But we finally seemed to be in sync.

Every week, I thought I would be eliminated from *DWTS*, because we were often in the bottom two of the results. I was frustrated, but then I started to hear from some of the more veteran *DWTS* crew, who told me that being among the last couples to find out our results didn't necessarily mean we were in the bottom two of voting. I was told I kept being placed there because I was good for ratings. The producers were dragging out the drama.

Maks and I made it through to week nine. I was in the final four—something I never would have expected when I signed the contract. I felt really good about my accomplishment.

On that last Monday night, we had to perform three dances. One was a difficult Argentine tango—it was physically taxing and full of lifts. We were the only dancers athletic enough to perform such a demanding routine. We knew it was one of our best. Of course, the judges were critical and sounded as though they were saying good-bye. "I really admired you for coming this far," Carrie Ann Inaba said.

When I heard that, I knew the next night would be our last.

When we were eliminated, I did one interview

with Tony Dovolani, who was one of the dancers on the show, working for *Extra*. He had become my friend, and he said some beautiful things to me when I came over for the interview—that I was his role model and he wanted his daughters to be like me. It hit me right then how far I had come—I had just wanted to give women's soccer some exposure, yet I had made it to the final four on *Dancing with the Stars*. I got very emotional and started to cry. Because of that, my PR person thought it was best if I didn't do any more interviews.

My time as Cinderella was over. My trailer was turning into a pumpkin. We packed up, and the next day, I flew home to Seattle, wearing my Nikes and my real eyelashes.

Grandpa Pete passed away in December, and my family gathered in Richland to say good-bye. He was our patriarch, the one who had moved us to eastern Washington and set my family on its journey. He had been my staunchest supporter, traveling the world to see me play and always encouraging me to be the best I could be. He could always make me laugh; when things got too serious or scary in my life, Grandpa Pete would crack a joke.

After the funeral, we released doves into the cold wind blowing off the Columbia River. I looked around at my family and at Adrian. I had always thought my grandpa might walk me down the aisle. He wouldn't be there to do that now, but I felt I had finally found the person I was going to make my life with, the person who had been right there for so many years.

New Year's Eve came two weeks later. At about eleven-thirty that night, my phone rang. It was Grandma Alice. "This is the first time in my entire eighty-four years that I've rung in the New Year by myself," she said.

When I told Adrian what she'd said, he jumped up. "Come on," he said.

We rushed to the house on Hoxie and gathered up Marcus, Johnny, Mom, and the ice-cream pie I had gotten for her birthday, then we hurried the four blocks to Grandma's house. We stepped past the sign that read GRANDKIDS WELCOME and found Grandma in the bedroom she had shared for so many years with Grandpa Pete. There was only a minute to spare in the old year. We sang "Happy Birthday" to my mother and toasted to 2012.

We stayed in Grandma's warm room playing Cranium until two a.m., Adrian and Marcus against me and Grandma, who kept trying to cheat. My mother held Johnny, asleep in her arms, and laughed at our crazy antics. Outside the wind blew off the Columbia, its waters rushing past us and out into the sea.

Grandma Alice looked out the window into the dark night.

"God's second paradise," she said with a smile.

The year 2012 is all about the London Olympics.

In January, we headed up to Canada for the CONCACAF Olympic qualifying tournament.

Our team is a wonderful mix of veterans and up-and-comers. It's amazing to see the teamwork and heart between us all.

It was only four minutes into the first game. Abby head-flicked the ball to Alex, who ran it up the field to give us an early lead. Later on, Alex assisted on two more goals by Abby. A second goal by Alex in the last half of the game solidified the win. With my two saves, the final score was 4–0.

By the end, we'd outscored our opponents by a combined score of 38–0 over five games. But, most importantly, we were headed to London.

On July 25, in Glasgow, Scotland, we faced France in our first game of the 2012 Olympics, two days before the official opening ceremonies. Our other opponents were Colombia, North Korea, New Zealand, Canada, and finally Japan.

I had three shutouts, two against Colombia with 3–0 and North Korea with 1–0, and a 2–0 win against New Zealand in the quarterfinal, and was one of three players on the team who played all 570 minutes in all 6 matches.

On August 9, I won my second Olympic gold medal defeating Japan 2–1 in the final match. It was an incredible day, and we were up against Japan, who had defeated us in the 2011 World Cup final in a penalty shootout. The stakes were high. The U.S.–Japan final drew a crowd of over 80,200 to London's Wembley Stadium, the largest ever to see a women's soccer game at the Olympics.

Carli Lloyd scored early in both halves and we played aggressively throughout. In the final minutes, Mana Iwabuchi stripped the ball from Christie and took a powerful shot which could have tied the match. I knew I had to make that save. I lunged left to deflect the ball and powerfully punched it away. We won the gold medal and redemption from our 2011 World Cup loss to Japan, and all rushed the field. President Obama posted his congratulations on Twitter.

The Olympics are the ultimate thrill, and I was hungry to compete again. It's felt like I've been on a long, long journey home.

Life isn't like a book. There's no way to tell in life when it's the beginning and when it's the end. Maybe beginnings and endings don't really exist. Just moments. And while I'm still not sure I believe in happy endings, I definitely believe in happy moments. Every morning, I wake up feeling blessed. I'm filled with graciousness to be able to travel the world, live life to the fullest, and play the game I love.

ACKNOWLEDGMENTS

WRITING AN HONEST BOOK MEANS that family secrets and private moments are exposed for the world to see. So first and foremost I want to thank my family, who have been unconditionally loving and supportive through both the good times and the rough spots. The process of bringing my story to print required unearthing some painful memories, but I share them here in the hope that something constructive might come from them. My family's courage and faith know no bounds, and I thank them for providing the foundation for my own path to happiness. Reality has tested us, but love has saved us. Here's to our beautiful struggle—Judy and Glenn Burnett; Marcus and Debbie Solo and their son, Johnny; David Solo; Terry and Christian Obert; Grandma Alice and my late Grandpa Pete.

And to my dad, who taught me to never give up.

Life has blessed me with many teachers and guiding influences who have, in their own ways, each contributed to the writing of this book.

To my family and friends, who have enriched my life in more ways than I can express: Mary and Dick Gies, Cheryl Hirss, Liz and Nan Duncan. Aunt Susie, Uncle Frank, and all of my cousins. Anita and Bob Galaviz, Uncle Raul, Jeff Obert, Carli Lloyd, Sofia Palmqvist, James Galanis, Tina, Mya, and MacKenzie Ellertson. My St. Louis family—the Owenses, Tim Owens, Tony Hubert and Jeff Cooper. Malia Arrant. Lesle Gallimore and Amy Griffin. And to other friends who I may have failed to mention here by name but who I hold in my heart with continued love, gratitude, and respect.

To my soccer family: my youth coaches Tim Atencio and Carl Wheeler. Pia Sundhage, Cheryl Bailey, Paul Rogers, April Heinrichs, Phil Wheddon, Sunil Gulati, Dan Flynn, and my teammates past and present.

Without the help of an unbelievable medical team,

I couldn't have gotten back on the field to experience the fulfillment of a World Cup and the thrill of another Olympic Games. Thanks to Dr. James Andrews and his medical team (Butch Buchanan, Luke Miller, and Harrison Reich) led by Kevin Wilke.

And to my rock Bruce Snell, Dave "Supe" Andrews, Ivan Pierra, and, of course, Hughie O'Malley.

To all my sponsors who have helped me in immeasurable ways, and, in particular, to Joe Elsmore and all my friends at Nike for their continued support.

To Richard Motzkin, for his longtime guidance and support, and to the indefatigable Whitney Unruh, for her friendship and for always knowing how to get the best out of me. She read me as closely as she read this book and was my rock solid. Rich and Whitney's dedication and hard work go beyond the call of duty, and I owe them a special debt of gratitude.

Completing the book is a testament to the talents and involvement of a great many people. Thank you to all the staff at HarperCollins, for their support and patience.

To Adrian, a blessing in my life. Thank you for strengthening my confidence in myself and for encouraging me to remain true to who I am at all costs. You have believed in me in ways that nobody else ever has. Our love is a love that builds a deep and unbreakable bond, no matter what challenges and heartache come our way. Some things were never possible without you by my side. We can do anything together. I love you.

QUESTIONS AND ANSWERS

1. Did you always know you wanted to be a soccer player?

Hope Solo: Yes—when I was twelve, my teacher asked us to write a paper about what we wanted to be when we grew up. I wrote that I wanted to be a professional soccer player, even though there was no women's professional soccer at that time.

2. What are the most important things to do to be a great goalie?

Hope Solo: Most people think goalkeeping is all about having good hands, but I focus on footwork in order to be speedy and agile in goal.

3. How did you feel when you got on to the Olympic soccer team?

Hope Solo: It was a lifelong dream of mine to play in the Olympics, so when I actually made the team I was filled with so much joy.

4. Which is more exciting: the Olympics or the World Cup?

Hope Solo: The Olympics and the World Cup are exciting in different ways. The World Cup is exciting because it's all about soccer and is the highest achievement in the sport. And the Olympics are exciting because of the camaraderie among all the different athletes and countries.

5. How has the popularity and image of soccer changed since you were a kid? How do you think it will change in the future?

Hope Solo: In my lifetime I have seen Major League Soccer (MLS) start and develop into a strong league with many followers. It's clear that soccer is one of the fastest-growing sports in the United States, and I envision that one day hopefully soccer will surpass America's favorite pastime sports like football and baseball. Soccer is the world's game.

6. If you could play a game of soccer with one legendary player, who would it be?

Hope Solo: If I could play a game of soccer with any legendary player, it would be Diego Maradona because I like his crazy personality.

7. What advice do you have for kids who want to be professional soccer players?

Hope Solo: Embrace your individual talents and realize that not everyone has the same gift on the field. But if you can find out what your gift is, then that is what will set you apart from everyone else.

8. If you weren't a soccer player, what would you want to be?

Hope Solo: If I weren't a soccer player, I would want to be a professional beach volleyball player.

9. What is your favorite thing to do when you're not playing soccer?

Hope Solo: I grew up on the river, so when I have the opportunity to get on a boat, that's when I find I'm the happiest.

10. Who is your biggest inspiration?

Hope Solo: My family is my biggest inspiration because they have influenced my life in more ways than anybody else has.

11. What do you do to prepare before a big game?

Hope Solo: Before a big game, I make sure that my emotions are not too high or too low. I don't listen to music that overly pumps me up, because I want to be in a composed mental state when I step on the field.

12. What was the best advice you ever received?

Hope Solo: One of my former coaches once told me,

"Let not your behavior off the field dictate where you go."

13. What is something your fans may not know about you?

Hope Solo: When I was a kid, I had a rabbit named Thumper. His teeth never stopped growing, so my mom and I had to cut them.

14. You're known for speaking your mind and standing up for yourself. Is this something you were always good at or something you learned to do?

Hope Solo: I am not an outspoken person and am actually pretty shy. But I do believe that everyone needs to take a stand when it's something worth fighting for.

15. We know that you've been involved in antibullying campaigns. Were you ever bullied?

Hope Solo: When I was younger, I was bullied for being a tomboy with braces who always wore soccer clothes. But I never let the bullying deter me from my dream.